THE TRUTH
ABOUT
LYING

WHY AND HOW
WE ALL DO IT
AND WHAT TO DO ABOUT IT

Table of Contents

Introduction xiii
The Lies that Triggered My Own Interest

Part I: The Social Context for Lying

The Pervasiveness of Lying 3
Determining the Lie . . .
How Animals and Plants Deceive . . .
The Trickster Figure in Human Myth . . .
The Morality & Social Dynamics of Lying . . .

Why the Lie? The Reasons and Justifications for Lying.............. 15
Types of Lies . .
The Reasons for Lying . .
Justifying the Lie . . .
Reactions to the Lies of Others . . .

Part II: Lying in Public and Professional Life

Everyday Social Lies.. 41
Covering up Real Feelings & Opinions . . .
Creating a Better Image or Appearance . . .
Avoiding Unpleasant or Undesirable Contacts . . .
Little Lies . . .

Lying in Public.. 49
Who Is Most Likely to Lie? .
Lying to Neighbors . . .

Lying at Work 55
Organizational Lies . . .
Employer Lies . .
Setting the Tone . . .
Lying by Employees . . . *To Get a Job or Promotion . . . To Make
Excuses or Cover up Delays, Lack of Work, & Mistakes . . . To
Obtain a Forbidden Goal or Take Advantage . . . To Gain Alter-
nate Goals or Priorities . . .*
Lying by Co-workers & Colleagues . . .
Gaining a Competitive Advantage . . .
Undermining Other Employees . . .

Lying in Business 69
Lies to Look Good . . .
Taking Credit &MakingCan-Do-ItClaimsWhenOneCan't
Lies for Revenge . .
The Case for Honesty & Ethics in Business . . .

Table of Contents

Part III: Lying in Personal & Private Life

7. *Lying to Friends & Relatives* 79
  Lying to Friends . . . *Lies to Help & Protect . . . Lies to Embel-
  lish & Entertain . . . Lack of Dependability & Follow-up Lies . . .
  Money Lies . . . Lies to End the Friendship . . .*
  Lying to Relatives . . .
  Lies of Avoidance . . .
  Lies to Impress . . .
  Lies about Money, Jealousy, & Revenge . . .

8. *When Men & Women Lie: The Dating Game* 95
  Lies to Yourself . . .
  Lies to Avoid Getting Involved in the Relationship . . . *Getting
  out of Dates . . . Lies to Avoid Intimacy . . .*
  Lies to Exaggerate, Show off, & Increase Self-Esteem .
  Persuading by Use of Lies about What Others Do . . .
  Lies to Conceal an Important Truth about Oneself . . .
  Other Lies to Get Sex . . .
  Lies about Seeing Others . . .
  Lies in the Heat of Passion . . .
  Lies about Seeing Others . . .
  Mixing Lies, Love, & Money . .
  Lies in Fights . . .
  The Response to Lies . . .
  The Desire for & the Dangers of Honesty . .

9. *Lies with Husbands, Wives, & Intimate Others* 127
  Lies & Sex . . .
  Lying & Affairs . . .
  Types of Concealments & Justifications . .
  Revealing & Reaction to the Lie . . .
  Lies to the Other Man or the Other Woman . . .
  Lies when the Marriage Ends . . .

  The Lies of Parents & Children.................................... 147
  What Parents Tell Children about Lying . . .
  When Parents Lie . . . *Lies to Protect Feelings . . . Lies to Con-
  ceal Opinions or Disapproval to Avoid Undue Influence . . .
  Lies to Conceal Inappropriate Information . . Lies to Get a
  Child to Do Something or Not Do Something .*
  When Children Lie . . . *Lies to Escape Punishment . . Lies to
  Conceal Unapproved Activities . . . Lies to Impress . . .
  Teenage Dating Lies . . . Lies to Help & Protect Others .*

Table of Contents

Lying to Oneself..163
Why the Self-Lie . . . *Lying about One's Own Abilities or One's Business* . . .
The Effects of Self-Lying in Relationships . . .
Lying to Oneself about Personal Problems & Limitations . . . Overcoming the Self-Lie . .

The Strategy of Deceiving & Perceiving...........................175
The Success of Deception . . .
The Strategies for Telling a Lie . . .
The Strategies for Perceiving a Lie . . . *Discovering Leakages... Discovering Deception Clues* . . . *Discovering Clues in the Overall Social Context*
Clues to Look for . . .

Conclusion...189
To Confront or Not to Confront the Lie? . . *Is the Confrontation Worth It?* . . .
The Importance of Being Diplomatic or Tactful . . .
When to Confess or What to Do about Getting Caught . . *Some Considerations in Whether to Lie* . . . *When to Reveal or Confess the Lie* . . . *The Role of Forgiveness* . . .
Toward a Solution in Dealing with Lying . . *Look at the Whys Behind the Lie* . . *Be Ready to Call People on Their Lies* . . . *Create a Supportive Environment for Truth Telling* . . . *Tell the Truth to Yourself* . . . *Use the Truth for Building & Healing Relationships* . . .
Recognize the Long-term Advantages of Being Committed to the Truth.

What's Your Lie-Q?...203

References...207

The Truth about Lying

IN RECENT YEARS, WE HAVE BEEN FACING A CRISIS of conscience over the ethical state of our nation. We have been going through a national soul-searching and judging, assessing ourselves in light of traditional core values of honesty and ethics, and reviewing and purging many fundamental institutions in revulsion to a decade of greed and excess. Why? Because we have seen more and more indications that acts of lying, deception, and other unethical deeds for short-term gain and personal advantage may have deeper, more serious consequences in undermining the bonds of trust that create relationships and community and give strength to the nation as a whole.

The examples leap from the pages of newspapers today. The insider-trading scandals that have wracked Wall Street and resulted in the sentencing of a parade of formerly highly esteemed individuals and firms that milked the system—Ivan Boesky, Drexel Burnham Lambert, Michael Milken. The Irangate hearings and trial of Oliver North, ultimately convicting and tarnishing the image of a former "hero" who ran secret operations and lied to

Congress. The votes-for-sale scandal in California that recently resulted in the conviction of lawmaker Mike Montoya, sentenced to six years in prison. The trials and conviction of federal judge Robert Aguilar for using his position to help friends and associates convicted of felonies. The conviction of Leona Helmsley, the New York hotel queen, for income-tax evasion. And the revelations of the lies and frauds by now-convicted and sentenced religious leader Jim Bakker, who for years and years beguiled funds from his followers in the name of God.

At the same time, there have been thousands of big-buck lawsuits fueled by claims of lies and duplicity, one of the most notable arising from the Challenger space-shuttle disaster. The widow of astronaut Mike Smith charged wrongful death, negligence, and duplicity within NASA, between contractors and the government, and between individuals and the government, leading to the errors and failures that produced the crash. Plus, there have been individual acts of desperation and deception by outwardly respectable people that have shocked the nation—as in the case of the Boston hoaxer, Charles Stuart, who tried to point the finger of guilt for the murder of his wife at a poor black man, then killed himself as the truth started to come out, suggesting he had done it for the insurance money. Even as I write this, there have been revelations of the secret life of a respected college president— Richard Berenzden of American University in Washington—who stepped down after a series of obscene calls was traced to his personal phone at the school, a case compared in the media to the web of lies covering up the secret life of another prominent Washingtonian—Mayor Marion Barry—filmed in a hotel room smoking cocaine.

More and more surveys and reports have been coming out, reflecting both a collective decline in ethical and honest behavior and a concern that this situation is a threat to our society.

For example, in 1987, a *U.S. News and World Report-CNN* poll found that more than half of the Americans surveyed thought that people were less honest than they had been ten years earlier and 71 percent said they were dissatisfied with the current standards of honesty. The poll also showed an especially high suspicion of public figures—only about one-third of the respondents thought their congressional leaders or the president would always or almost always tell the truth.' In addition, there was low confidence in the media, since only 38 percent of the respondents thought the daily newspapers almost always tell the truth. In fact, the poll showed the level of general dissatisfaction with the nation's honesty to be at its lowest point since an all-time low in 1973 right after the Watergate scandal—far below the much happier time in the 1963 survey, when only 58 percent of those polled expressed dissatisfaction.

In turn, a growing number of reports and public figures have been expressing this sad state of affairs. For example, this same *U.S. News* article reporting the poll noted that there had been a "rash of revelations about hyped and falsified scientific research," including a study published in January 1987 that accused 47 scientists at the medical schools of Harvard and Emory universities of producing misleading papers. Also, according to *U.S. News and World Report,* a House subcommittee in 1986 estimated that one out of every three working Americans was hired with educational or career credentials that were altered in some way. In another study, Ward Howell International, an executive headhunting firm, found that more than one in four executives reported that their organizations had hired employees whose "job qualifications, educational credentials, or salary history had been misrepresented."[2] And a poll of personnel executives done by *Personnel Journal* in 1987 indicated that over two-thirds of those responding felt that ethics would be an increasing problem in the future, noting a number of types of deceptions as examples of this growing trend, including falsifying expense accounts, misusing or misrepresenting the use of company-provided benefits, withholding important information, accepting bribes, concealing errors, and circumventing the rules.[3]

Meanwhile, the *U.S. News* article quoted a number of public figures and social scientists who observe a growing trend toward lying in public and personal life, or as former U.S. Representative Richard Boling has put it: "There is an attitude that seems very prevalent today—that if you can get away with it, go ahead and lie."[4] And the founder of the citizens' lobby Common Cause, John Gardner, has similarly observed that duplicity and deception in public and private life "are very substantially greater than they have been in the past."[5]

So why should all this be important? Simply because trust, born out of honesty and truth, is essentially the glue that holds personal relationships, communities, and societies together. The U.S. News-CNN poll found that 94 percent of the people questioned stated that honesty was an extremely important attribute or quality in a friend—in fact, it was the quality most highly agreed upon among many others listed (including looks, dress, appearance, intelligence, sense of humor, and common interests).[6] And when I did my own research, interviewing formally and informally dozens of people about their perceptions of lying in everyday life, I found broad agreement on the importance of honesty and integrity, combined with an awareness of the commonness of lying and its dangers. Though people might at times for various reasons engage in some lies themselves, they for the most part considered themselves to be honest, respectable, responsible.

Indeed, the more I thought about lying, the more I realized its complexities. On the one hand, if lying becomes more common and if people lose their confidence in each other or in national institutions as a result, there is a threat to the social contract in society that binds us together with others in relationships and groups. On the other hand, there are many reasons to lie, not only for personal advantage and gain, but to help or protect others, or even to facilitate the operations of ordinary social discourses (such as the white lie to give an acceptable excuse or comment, rather than tell a truth that might be hurtful or disruptive). Yet, while those who lie might feel the particular lie justified or appropriate, those experiencing the lie may not; they might rather know the truth, whatever the hurt.

But then would they really? The subject of lying comes in many shades of grey, though we all might admit that there is some kind of ethics crisis that has led a growing number of businesses to introduce ethics-training programs, universities to start classes and programs on ethics, law schools to introduce classes on professional responsibility, and individuals to start going to workshops on ethics and truth. I attended a workshop at Esalen, the well-known growth center in Big Sur, California, in the course of writing this book. The workshop was on examining the truth and was titled "Living an Authentic Life: Implications of Truth-telling."[7]

The Lies That Triggered My Own Interest

What led me to become interested in this topic? Basically, it was a series of incredibly outrageous lies that I encountered. They undermined my own sense of trust in everyday social relationships and I didn't know how to handle them. Then, too, as I reflected on my own experiences, I realized there were times when I, like many of the other business and professional people I knew, engaged in everyday sorts of favorable presentations of self to gain a business or professional advantage. Were these lies? Deceits? Concealments? Or had these become part of the everyday rules of business success and image creation?

The first lie that led me to start wondering about lying occurred when I was working for an apparently successful travel promoter. I met him in the fall of 1983, after I saw an ad in the paper for tour escorts. It would be fun to lead a tour and be paid for it, or at least receive a free trip, I thought, and I scheduled an interview at a small office in Alameda, just across the bay from San Francisco at the edge of Oakland. The promoter, whom I'll call Rex King, was tall, slick, handsome, the very image of a successful travel magnate. He claimed he had been sent out by the big travel organization he headed on the East Coast to try a new concept in the West—organizing single people and sending them to romantic, exotic destinations where they would stay in beautiful luxury resorts.

So why use tour escorts? His thought, he explained, was to balance out the groups so there were equal numbers of men and women, The escorts wouldn't be paid; they would just have a free trip. They were to act like everyone else, and everyone would have fun.

It sounded like a great opportunity, even though I wondered why he needed women as escorts for a singles travel program, since my experience with singles travel groups was that they were mostly women. And would single women really feel comfortable being romanced by a paid escort?

Assuming that Rex knew what he was doing—after all, he had been in the business for a decade and had the million-dollar company back east behind him—I shut off my questions. Even when another woman who was interviewed at the same time— an attractive, vivacious brunette with a background in PR— speculated over coffee that maybe Rex really wanted to run prostitutes to Mexico and was using the tour-escorts ad as a cover, I dismissed her theories as wild speculation and paranoia. I concluded that Rex might simply be a little naïve about the West Coast singles market because he was new in town.

So what could be wrong? Maybe I just didn't want to see it. Why? Because I saw that this travel program could be a great opportunity, not just to be a tour escort, but to help Rex with what he really needed—someone to guide him with marketing on the West Coast. This seemed like just the step up I needed to use my sales expertise to help someone in launching a branch of a million-dollar company.

I regaled Rex with my thoughts, and drew up a marketing plan. He began inviting me to sales and promotional meetings. He had business cards made up in my name. My title was "Marketing Director." It had a nice ring, and Rex's talk about building a close-knit sales family had a nice ring, too. It was also reassuring to be part of a growing new venture, backed by what Rex described as a $38-million corporation with branch offices in 21 cities. And when Rex handed me my first check for about $1,000 to cover the marketing plans and scripts for a slide show I wrote, I was even more reassured. What could go wrong?

As Rex reached out for customers, his partner Jerry, a serious accountant type, worked on the other side of the business in an office down the hall, trying to set up incentive and premium trips for businesses. He even set up a few trips for doctors and lawyers while I was there. Meanwhile, Rex had recruited about two dozen attractive tour escorts, both men and women, in their twenties and thirties. So everything seemed on the level.

Rex's efforts at landing customers started with a big party at a popular restaurant. There were slides of exotic locations, plenty of hors d'oeuvres, drinks on the house, about sixty glamorous people, including several bankers Rex was talking to about extra funding, a few press people, a couple of investors, and the heads of several local singles clubs. Of course there also were several dozen single people who were the potential market for this program, plus about a dozen of the tour escorts hired through the interviews. I had also helped Rex and his staff—which now included Sheri, a glamorous former lingerie model who had become his chief administrative assistant, and Jerry—put together fliers about the planned trips, emphasizing the romance and glamour of these beautiful resorts. Sheri had put together a list of trip schedules.

All still seemed fine. Rex made his gala entrance and introduced his staff and his concept. Everyone seemed impressed, and soon Rex and his lingerie-model assistant were flying off to this resort or that, presumably checking the facilities, with the trips subsidized by the airlines or resorts that wanted his business. Also there were reams of postcards going out to singles who had responded to ads describing the trips.

The only problem was, no one was signing up for trips. Rex even collected membership fees from people interested in his new singles travel organization, which would include discounts on parties and trips. But, despite the list of scheduled trips, there were still no sign-ups.

That would be just a matter of time, Rex kept assuring us. The first party had been just a way to say hello to everyone, to show off this wonderful new singles travel organization. What was needed now was another party to produce these sign-ups.

Once again, plans for a party were launched. As planning for the next glittery party continued, I started to notice some of the warning signs. A check given to me bounced, but Rex assured me it was just a glitch at the bank. But in a few days he had changed banks and then, he said, he needed just a few more days for the funds to clear. A week later I still wasn't paid, but he had still more reassuring stories. A check was coming from the home office that would make everything good. And so on.

Soon there were other signals. I introduced Rex to a friend who ran a newspaper, and Rex arranged for a singles ad. But Rex said he left his checkbook behind and would send the money. Now, two months later, after the ad appeared, my friend told me Rex never had paid. Could I do anything to help him get his money? Rex assured me that payment would be on its way shortly.

This pattern of delay and excuses continued for a couple of months, with more and more people arriving with stories of promised payments that never arrived, checks that bounced and weren't made good, investors who never got statements about the company's earnings or expenses. Meanwhile, as if nothing were wrong, the mailings continued, memberships in this supposed singles organization were accepted, and finally, the last, largest, and most lavish party was planned. It would be a singles travel party, with several singles organizations setting up booths. Rex even talked the center where the event would be held into accepting payment the night of the party, though normally it demanded at least 50 percent down. The caterer, the band, everyone else involved, agreed to be paid that night. Rex was confidently predicting 300, 400 people. It was to be, he said, the culmination of his dreams and hopes. He appeared at the event in a shiny white suit, surrounded by his glamorous women groupies, looking like some tropical potentate or god.

That's when it all exploded. Rex had been promising to pay me that night for my previous work—though this was now three months after the first promises. I had taken the precaution of filing a small-claims suit, and I had a friend at the party, ready to serve him with the suit if he declined to pay.

Rex not only didn't pay me and was served by my friend that night, but he didn't pay dozens of other people, either, including the caterer, band, or anyone else. Instead, after the event turned into an unmitigated disaster—with only about 150 people there at just $10 each—there was no way for it to break even, much less make money. So, later that night, quite drunk and with the cash actually received in hand, Rex calmly wrote out about $15,000 in checks to the center, the caterer, the band, and several others. But the next day he closed his account, which had only about $3,000 in it anyway. A few days later, he abandoned his office and left town, leaving about $45,000 in bills and a lot of people in deep shock.

Piece by piece, the story started to come out. As a result of lawsuits filed by me and about a dozen others in small-claims court—which prompted a series of articles in the local newspaper—some criminal charges concerning bad checks and fraud were filed by the Alameda and San Francisco District Attorney's offices. Rex was arrested about a week later in southern California as a result of making a faulty left turn at a traffic stop. The police officer found a credit-card imprinter belonging to someone else in the back seat of Rex's car, leading to more investigations.

Eventually, Rex was transferred back to Alameda county and served time in jail, though his lawyer arranged for him to pay restitution for one of the check charges in the strongest case in return for two years' probation. Then Rex left town again, leaving behind perhaps $40,000 in civil claims.

And what of the glorious, $38-million company with its twenty-one branches? As it turned out, there wasn't any. Rex had perhaps sold tours for a travel company back East, and he had taught some courses on travel at a local travel school where he met Jerry. In reality, he had come West to seek his fortune, for a while had lived with a woman he had met, and then had moved into an unfurnished apartment in Alameda with Jerry. They were both so poor that they slept on mattresses. As it turned out, they didn't even have a phone there or pay their rent, either.

Rex was a good talker, and he had roped in a good investor in the beginning—someone I knew, which helped to give the operation credibility. That's where the money to pay me and for the ads had come from.

Did Rex set out to be a con artist? Was what happened all part of a plot to defraud? I don't think so. I think Rex probably started out with good intentions. But to make that dream happen, he lied to build himself up, to give himself the credibility and reputation he needed. As plans failed, as others didn't respond to his dream, as the money didn't come in, Rex didn't stop to pull out, he didn't do a reality check. Instead, he kept furnishing his dream with still more hopes, and then, because reality didn't nourish them, he kept watering those hopes with more lies.

That was just the first big lie I experienced. The second seemed even bigger—and I lost even more.

It all started innocently enough in the early spring of 1985, about two years after the travel program with Rex fell apart. I had developed doll ideas with a doll designer whom I'll call Sarah, and we had signed a contract with a small national company to produce them. I was also working as a writer, and I had left some of my brochures at a social gathering sponsored by the San Francisco Chamber of Commerce.

I got a call from a man whom I'll call Richard. He had seen my brochure and was looking for a partner to seek an educational contract. He had a background in education, he said, and needed someone to help write the proposal. As we talked about collaboration, he mentioned that he was trying to get a children's book he had written published. I mentioned the dolls. In fact, I said, I had written a children's book based on them, and would he like to see it? Sure, he said, and so our star-crossed venture began.

Soon, the idea of a collaboration on an educational project was left behind. Richard was excited about my children's book based on the dolls, which at that time I called the Little Devils. They had been inspired by my research in shamanism, which involved studying with a shaman who would go out into the countryside and work in the darkness, calling on the forces of nature. This gave me the idea for some dolls that represented the mischievous or unpredictable qualities of nature. Sarah, the doll designer, had helped to turn these ideas into cute, sprightly characters. My book was about how these little creatures might pop up just about everywhere.

Richard found the idea charming. In fact, he was so excited that he said he would put his own book idea on the shelf and publish my book first. His proposal seemed like a dream from heaven. It was the perfect tie-in to help promote these dolls, and he assured me he had the publisher and artist lined up.

As is often the case, it took me a while to realize I was being lied to, because, as I later discovered in my research on lying, it is far easier to lie than for the receiver to perceive the lie.

So the chain of lies I followed began. At first, everything seemed quite normal, though in retrospect, I realize I might have seen warnings along the way. Richard brought over a book contract for me to sign, explaining that he hoped to keep things informal and friendly, without any lawyers, and I agreed. Then he seemed a little unclear about how much my royalty would be. "It is my first book, and I want to do what's fair," he explained, and finally we came up with a figure based on what I had received for other books.

So far, so good, I thought, but then, slowly, step-by-step, the changes began. The first came soon after Richard introduced me to the illustrator for my book. The samples of her previous works looked great, as did a few rough sketches of illustrations for my book. But a few days later, Richard informed me that he had decided to find another illustrator because he thought her whimsical sketches looked too deformed. "But it will just cost us a few days' delay," he assured me. Sarah agreed.

Richard then suggested other changes. He worried about the name of the dolls—the Little Devils. Would this offend the Christian market? I tried to explain that most people thought the dolls were humorous, mischievous little figures of *fun;* but he told me his "people" thought the name would hurt sales. I agreed to talk to the doll manufacturer to see what the company head and the national sales manager thought. "Call them whatever you want," they responded.

Then Richard had other concerns. Now, he said, his "people" were worried about the devil tails on the dolls. Even if the name were changed, the tails still suggested "Little Devils," and his "people" thought this should be changed. I talked to the doll manufacturer, and again they were willing to go along. They were excited by the prospect of a book based on the dolls and the possibility of selling the two together, so again they told me, "Sure, do whatever you want to do."

Richard proposed still more changes, and soon he was calling the doll manufacturer directly, as well as reviewing his thoughts with the doll designer. The manufacturer wasn't sure whether to deal with him directly, but I said go ahead. When his illustrator came up with a different face for the dolls, the manufacturer seemed willing to go along. "Just send us the final images in time for us to make models for our catalog," the manufacturer said.

As this was going on, a few weeks before the catalog deadline in early April, Richard had suggestions for my story. His "people" thought it was too long and had too many characters. And besides, it might seem more believable and realistic if . . He listed a few changes he wanted. Because I said I was busy with other deadlines, he told me not to worry. He would make the changes he suggested and show me a draft. But when I saw it, I hardly recognized my original story. My fantasy characters had taken a little boy off to a secret world of adventure. But the fantasy characters in this story had appeared to help the boy celebrate a birthday. "Oh, don't worry about it. You'll still get the credit and the royalty for this," said Richard.

I was stunned. It was as if Richard were inviting me to put my name on someone else's story. At the time I felt I had no choice, because he was the publisher.

The only problem, as I later found out, was, there was no book. It was only a dream in Richard's eye, because he did not have the money to publish any book. The "people" he spoke of so grandly as part of his publishing company were really just a husband-and-wife team who ran a small contract publishing venture and were going to publish the book only if they were paid. In the middle of these negotiations Richard had lost his paying sales-rep job for a big company, and he had been stringing the publishers along for about six weeks, promising payments that didn't come. His new "illustrator," whose art was supposed to define the final look of these dolls, was just an elementary-school teacher who did amateurish black-and-white sketches.

Unfortunately, when I agreed to Richard's latest request for changes, we were also just days away from the manufacturer's catalog deadline. Supposedly, the dolls now had a new name, a new story, and new characteristics. But what of the final art? "Don't worry," Richard assured me and the manufacturer. His artist was working on it and he would rush the art to the manufacturer in time.

About two days before the deadline, Richard, agitated and upset, appeared at my house with the doll designer. He spoke darkly of how the publisher he had trusted was trying to take the manuscript and publish it himself and was withholding the art. But he and Sarah had just been to a lawyer. He had written a strong letter to the printer threatening a suit if the art and manuscript were not returned, and Richard was confident the problem would be resolved successfully.

I was confused. Why hadn't Richard told me directly? Why had he and the doll designer seen a lawyer?

Besides, Richard hinted darkly, now that he and the designer were working together and there had been all of these changes, it was hard to say whose dolls or story these were anymore. He didn't come right out and say it, but there was the implication that maybe my contract with the manufacturer and the copyright on the original dolls no longer covered the new dolls and story. "You just provided the concept," said the doll designer, "but I made the dolls, and you acted as my agent in selling them." "But then," Richard quickly added, "we really want to be fair. We don't want to try to take anything from you. Even if the ownership and copyright are unclear, you would still get the same 5050 split on the dolls under your contract with the manufacturer and the royalty on the book. Even if I did a lot of rewriting, I still want to give you that. So we're not taking anything away from you, and we just all need to stick together."

Richard's proposal hit me like a brick. He was claiming to be fair. We're not taking anything away from you, he had said. Yet the underlying, sinister message from the two of them was that if I didn't agree to go along and not contact the manufacturer, I might lose my claim to the dolls and the book entirely for there had been all these changes. Taken together, they had totally transformed the original concept of the dolls. They had turned the original mischievous little creatures I imagined into something bland; and I thought Richard's rewrite of my story was simpering and dull.

Reluctantly, concealing my anger, I agreed to Richard's proposal. Yet I could hardly believe the transaction and felt totally betrayed, not only by Richard, but also by the doll designer. I realized I had made this whole thing possible by wanting to be fair myself. I had originally paid the doll designer to make models for me; and though I didn't have to, I had offered her 50 percent of the returns for selling the designs. Now, inspired by Richard, she had decided she had been the creator of the dolls and I was just the agent.

Looking back, I realize I could have stopped the process and stepped out of the web of lies by telling the manufacturer that it looked as if the book and art might not be done on schedule, so let's go back to the original concept. Instead, I felt I had no power because I had let Richard and the doll designer take it all away, since I feared that if I tried to do anything I would only lose it all.

Thus, as Richard and the doll designer asked, I did nothing, and for weeks I was too furious with the doll designer to even ask her where she stood. I just assumed she fully understood and agreed to what was going on, although later I discovered that Richard had lied to her, too.

In the end Richard missed the art deadline, so the manufacturers didn't put the dolls in their catalog and eventually decided not to do them at all. Richard never did publish any book.

It was only a few months later when I spoke to the printing company Richard worked with and about a year later to the doll designer that the whole truth came out. In reality, the printers were not trying to steal any manuscripts or illustrations from Richard; they just weren't going to publish anything unless Richard paid for costs to date. The art wasn't publication quality anyway, just the amateurish line drawings that one of the printers showed me when I met with her to find out what had gone on. Later, when I met with the designer, she told me how Richard had convinced her that the only way the dolls would come out is if there was a book, and then he had even suggested that she drop the arrangement with me entirely. As she told me, "He said I was only getting 50 percent under the current contract. Wouldn't I like to get 100 percent?" She didn't think that was right, so they made the offer they did.

The whole thing unraveled because the book itself was only a fantasy and Richard had pulled both me and the designer into it with all his lies. When reality finally set in, as in the case with Rex, all hopes collapsed, and for a while I felt a sense of numbness and shock. How could someone do this? Richard didn't even apologize or express remorse. He didn't even seem to realize what he had done wrong or have any awareness or concern about the wake of destruction he left in his path.

For me it was a powerful lesson about the destructive power of lies and the need to be cautious in knowing whom and how and when to trust. I have moved on to create other dolls and children's stories, and have avoided the same kind of traps, but I still have the Little Devils sitting on my shelves as a reminder.

About two years ago, I had my third encounter with the big lie, which finally inspired my research and this book. In this case, I did detect the lie. But I was puzzled in deciding what to do about it. Should I confront it? Should I bring it out in the open? Should I help the person I was certain was lying save face? Should I act as if I didn't know when I knew?

What happened was this: I had ghostwritten an article for a long-term client. He was a friend of other clients, in fact, referred by them, and he referred me to others. There had been no problem until he gave me incorrect instructions about something he wanted me to write. When he discovered the error, he wanted me to rewrite the project. Sure, I told him and quoted the cost. At first he resisted. He thought I should just write it again, because it was wrong. He tried to suggest it had been my fault, so I should do this for free. When I pointed out his wrong instructions, he proposed I do it for half price. After I explained I would have to start the project from scratch, he reluctantly agreed to pay the whole thing. So I went ahead.

A few days later, he arrived to pick it up. He reached into his pockets to pay, then pulled his empty hands out, saying he had forgotten his cash. "But I have a checkbook in the car," he said brightly, and, taking the manuscript, he went out to get it. About a minute later, he was back, saying he didn't have his checkbook, either. But he said he would come back with the money later that night.

What should I do? He waited for my response. In those moments, marked by an eerie stillness, as if truth were hanging in the balance, I knew—just knew to an absolute certainty—that this man was lying. And I knew why: He didn't want to assume the responsibility for the wrong instructions, even though he acknowledged them, because he didn't want to pay any more.

Could I really confront a client I had worked with for years and tell him he was lying? Would he even admit it if I did? Or was it better to just accept the immediate loss of money and hope for future gains?

The incident lingered with me, because I felt I was not only tricked by this lie, but I had *let* myself be tricked.

As I suspected, the man—I'll call him Jack—did not show up that night. When I called him the next day, he had an excuse. His car had broken down, he had been late, he couldn't get over. But tomorrow or the next day, he would be in San Francisco again, and then he would bring over the cash.

Needless to say, he did not, and over the next couple of weeks there were more promises made and broken. I never confronted him with my suspicions in order to get to the bottom of what happened and his reasons for doing it.

And I never was paid, although I did express my suspicions to his friends after he moved and got a new phone number, and I wasn't able to reach him. But all that did was feed his hostility toward me. It came in the form of whispered complaints about me to discourage other clients, and he never did ask me to write anything else for him again. For a long time, this resolution felt unsatisfying and incomplete because I hesitated to do what I really wanted to do in the first place—bring out the lie and talk about the reasons motivating it in order to achieve some mutually agreed upon resolution.

For me, healing came eventually through developing this book. In the travel program and doll scenarios, I hadn't been aware of the lies or had been unwilling to see them until too late. But in this case, I had been aware, and still I felt confounded and puzzled by the question of what to do. This led me to start thinking about the problem of lying in general. Can we tell when others lie? When do they? And when we know or suspect, what should we do?

This book reflects the results of these ruminations and my interviews with dozens of people formally and informally about their own experiences in lying or being lied to by others.

It begins with an overview of the pervasiveness of lying today and throughout time, then looks at the range of lies and reasons for lying. Following chapters deal with the different types of lies that occur in different situations—ranging from dealing with strangers, salespeople, and officials in everyday settings, to encounters with work and business associates, friends, relatives, parents, children, in dating relationships, and with spouses and intimate others. Also, the chapters in the last section deal with feelings about lying, strategies for lying and concealment, perceptions of lying, and what happens when people choose to confront and bring the lie out into the open.

The book concludes with chapters on what to do about all this yourself. What are guidelines for perceiving lies and accepting or confronting them? When is it appropriate to lie or deceive oneself? How can one reconcile lying and truth-telling with the conflicting needs for relationships based on trust and self-protection? And what do we need to do as a society to deal with these issues raised by lying in everyday life?

Part I

The Social Context
for Lying

CHAPTER 1

The Pervasiveness of Lying

*D*ESPITE THE RECENT OUTCRY against unethical behavior and lying in everyday life that can threaten the bonds that link human relationships and society as a whole, lying is ubiquitous. It goes back to the dawn of human history, is found in all human societies, and occurs throughout the animal kingdom—and even in some plants. Moralists, religious leaders, and philosophers decry it as ethically and morally wrong, as something that destroys trust, love, friendship, the social contract, and so forth. But as long as there have been societies—from the simplest to the most complex—there have been lies. Most basically, lies protect the individual. Sometimes they can be used to protect the individual's relationships, community, and national groups, too. Biologists even suggest that this capacity or propensity for lying has been wired into our genes as an adaptive mechanism that has helped us and other forms of life survive.

Just how pervasive is this thing called lying?

Determining the Lie

What is lying? People have different definitions, and "lying" can depend on how narrowly people define it.

In this book, I will be using the broadest, most inclusive definition. Then I will distinguish between more-serious and less-serious lies, sometimes referred to as "white lies," that are often an accepted part of everyday social discourse, sometimes a kind of social convention not even considered a lie by some.

For example, in her classic book on the moral implications of lying, Sissela Bok focuses on "clear-cut lies"—lies where the liar has an obvious intention to mislead, knows that what he is communicating is not what he believes, and where he has not deluded himself into believing the lie.' Others who have considered defining the lie have suggested it must involve some kind of misstatement disbelieved by the speaker, and then have argued about whether the intent of the speaker matters. Must he intend to deceive? Or might a misstatement be excused if it was said under duress? As a joke? As a bluff? For instance, in one such academic exercise, Thomas E. Carson rejects the usual definition that lying involves uttering a false statement or falsehood with the intent to deceive. He suggests that it can also involve uttering a deliberate false statement that is "foreseen to be likely to deceive others."[2] There have also been equally scholarly efforts to attempt to distinguish among lying; bluffing, which involves faking something rather than falsifying it; and "bull-shitting," which involves weaving a web of fakery that goes beyond bluffing in a particular situation to fake on a greater scale.[3]

Lying need not be confined to deceptive statements. It also can occur through behaviors—such as actions or gestures that are employed to support the lies—or concealments of relevant information, or just by making a promise or agreement without the intent to keep it. Out-and-out fabrications may thus be only a small part of lying in a broader sense of the word. From this angle, lying is ubiquitous—in animals and plants as well as in humans from the beginning of time.

How Animals & Plants Deceive

Whether animals have the actual ability to plan their acts of deception has long been a question among scholars. But there is no question that animals and many plants do engage in devious behavior. "At its most elementary level, deception is a protective strategy, woven into evolutionary design," according to a recent *U.S. News and World Report* article.[4] The use of camouflage in nature is a way to protect the organism through disguise so it will be less likely to be eaten by some eager predator. Examples from the insect kingdom include bugs that look like sticks or stones; moths with spots on their wings that look like owls' eyes; and Viceroy butterflies with the wing patterns of the poisonous Monarch butterfly. Supposedly, this deceit will make a bird think the insect is inedible and pass it by.'

Plants use their own ploys. They may be bright and beautiful to entice insects to come to help them disperse their pollen. In other cases, insect eaters such as the Venus fly trap entice and cajole with their beauty. Then when the insect enters, expecting a treat, the trap snaps shut.

Moving up in the animal kingdom, there are numerous examples of birds, such as the plover, that try to lure predators from their nests by pretending to have a broken wing or otherwise leading the predator on a wild-goose chase.'

Among primates, trickery becomes even more complex and more obviously planned and intentional, showing clearer parallels with the kinds of lies among humans. When R. W. Byrne and A. Whiten studied baboons, they found much deceptive behavior within the group seeking an advantage not just to get food but also to attain other goals, such as dominance or protection from attack. In one example, a young juvenile began screaming to suggest that an adult female who was digging for food was attacking him, with the result that his mother came and chased the other female away. With the adult female gone, the juvenile was able to eat her food.'

Likewise, reports by Jane Goodall about the chimpanzees she studied in the Gombe Reserve in Africa have provided numerous examples of deceitful behavior and tricks by chimps. Some of the less powerful adult males found that they could make others submit if they made loud noises by banging on pots or garbage-can lids from Goodall's camp. For a while this strategy made them the dominant males. But after the other chimps realized that these chimps had no special powers from these devices, they fought back, and the less powerful males soon were back to their former status.'

Biologists such as R. H. Wiley suggest that this deception has evolved because camouflage, mimicry, and intimidation contribute to the organism's survival.[9] Generally, because lying and deceit have proved to be adaptive, they have been programmed into our ancestry. We have learned to lie, because for survival,

lying works. Or as the social psychologists Charles Bond, Karen
Kahler, and Lucia Paolicelli have put it:

> Genetic capacities for deception have evolved through
> natural selection . . In conflicts between predator and
> prey, in struggles over scarce resources, deception con-
> fers a selective advantage. For hundreds of genera-
> tions, the less cunning have left behind fewer offspring,
> and deceptive capabilities have come to dominate the
> gene pool. Some of the resulting adaptations are ana-
> tomical (like coloration that offers concealment), while
> others are behavioral (like bird songs that mimic an
> opponent's rivals) . . . . Although we (may) marvel . . . at
> the wonders of animal dissimulation, *Homo sapiens* is
> the master of deceit, for the brain our ancestors evolved
> affords the most flexible deceptive repertoire . . a
> repertoire which is influenced by genetically transmitted
> differences in aptitude . . . [10]

Given this adaptive quality of lying, traced back to our animal
ancestry, is there any wonder there is so much lying today and
throughout human history?

According to Bond, Kahler, and Paolicelli, there seems to be
one other protection, forever locked in a struggle to combat the
individual lie—the ability of the person who is lied to to detect
lying has evolved as well. Why? Because "the liar gains evolutionary advantage at the dupe's expense, (so) dupes have left
behind fewer offspring, and an aptitude for lie detection has
evolved."[11] But that has led to a kind of evolutionary arms race
in which the dupes get better, but the liars adopt still newer and
better deceptive tactics for survival through natural selection.

The Trickster Figure in Human Myth

In many cultural traditions, the trickster figure has long been a
hero in story and myth. Possibly he was born in the ancient
hunting-gathering past, a person using his cleverness, trickery, and
deceit to lure game. A figure of a man with outstretched arms and
erect penis near a bison-like figure with a spear through it was
found in the famous cave of Lascaux in the Dordogne Valley of
France, and may represent a man engaged in hunting magic.

The basic image of the trickster is someone who goes after what
he or she wants through trickery and deceit and often suc-

ceeds or uses this trickery to help the culture as a whole. Sometimes, though, the trickster is fouled up by his or her own tricks.

A classic example of this archetype is the Coyote figure among native North Americans. In a typical story, he is presented as a selfish buffoon using tricks and deceits to gratify his "enormous appetites for food and sex." Because the elaborate deceits so often backfire, he ends up looking foolish.[12] He is very much a creature of the id, whom scholars have described as representing "the primordial creativity that exists in all of us," or as a "fun-loving, irreverent, crude, directly sexual, irresponsible, and unpredictable" character.° In other myths he is presented as the creator of the earth, the slayer of monsters, the teacher of cultural skills and customs, and a cultural transformer. According to scholar William Manson, these opposing themes in the trickster's character represent the tensions that exist within all individuals and society. One is the instinctual desire for gratification and the expression of powerful yet socially proscribed desires and fantasies. The second is the development of civilization and culture, based on controlling these desires." The trickster stories represent a playing out and reconciliation of these two impulses.

These devious heroes can take different forms. The image of Br'er Rabbit, from the southern black American folk tales, is still another example of the pervasiveness of this wily trickster, as is the fox and wolf in the folk tales of Western Europe and the spider and jackal in Africa.[15] The ancient Greeks had their own trickster in the person of Hermes, the Olympian messenger, who often tricked his way out of difficult situations. In Europe, the medieval jester and the irrepressible Tyl Eulenspiegel figure took this role.[16]

One can find in the Bible a whole cast of characters seeking to gain an advantage who used deceit because they had less power in general or in a particular situation. Many are women, such as Tamar and Judith, who combined their sexual wiles with deceitful speech, and Rebecca, who cagily schemed to win the first-born's blessing for Jacob from her husband.[17] Others are males, such as David, who used trickery not only to defeat Goliath, but later as king, to outwit his enemies and acquire Bathsheba, then the wife of another man.

As Naomi Steinberg and other scholars observe, "trickery is used by a person in a position of social disadvantage in order to influence the course of events."

There is still another function that long has been associated with deception and the trickster figure—the possibility of getting outside the strictures of society and escaping taboos.

For example, Joseph Epes Brown, a well-known authority on Plains Indian cultures, refers to the use of deception and trickery by trickster figures and clowns among American Indian groups as the "wisdom of the contrary." These figures do things in ways that break with traditional norms or they do things to fool people. If they go too far, they can be punished by their own tricks, such as happened to one medicine man, Black Elk, acting in the role of a trickster in a ceremony. He claimed he was going to make the earth rise in front of everybody within the tepee, as Brown tells the story. He put gunpowder just under the surface of the earth, and when he called on the earth to rise, he touched it off. The earth did rise. But the gunpowder flared up and singed his eyes, and from that time on, he was nearly blind. As the medicine man described it, he had been punished for trying to go too far in fooling people.[19]

Some scholars suggest that the trickster figure plays a key role in defining acceptable behavior since he is continually, unknowingly overstepping boundaries. When he goes too far, he is reined in. Ingvild Saelid Gilhus suggests that this figure reflects "the borderlines between order (and) lack of order in relationship to society, because the trickster shows an inability to recognize that structure and always acts against it."[20] Moreover, in some incarnations this trickster figure is transformed into a devil figure. For example, Gilhus suggests that the devil character within Christian gnosticism reflects this aspect of the devious trickster who sets himself up in opposition to God and the spiritual world and reflects the more material, biological, and animal qualities of the human being.[21] So while the trickster can be a hero who uses his wiles and can advance his culture as a source of innovation, in another aspect the trickster is a demonic figure that challenges the everyday order.

It is this central paradox and ambiguity of the trickster, so universal in human culture, that affects how we view lying in everyday life. We disparage the liar and the idea of deception. But at times the lie is necessary to help and protect, as in the whole category of social or white lies. And there are those who justify lying to advance a social good, such as to protect someone's life or to preserve a cherished value or the nation.

Also paradoxical is that lying appears to be part of our biological nature—we are programmed to lie; it's in our genes—while all societies denounce lying as being harmful to human relationships and the social order.

The Morality & Social Dynamics of Lying

How should we deal with lying? What lies are acceptable?

The ideal has been to speak the truth, particularly in the Judao-Christian tradition, where lying is viewed as morally wrong, evil, even a sin. Familiar quotes from the Bible speak of the virtues of truth: "Great is Truth, and mighty above all things" (Apocrypha 1, Esdras 4:41); "Rejoiceth not in iniquity, but rejoiceth in the truth" (Corinthians 13:1); "And ye shall know the truth, and the truth shall make you free" (St. John 32). On the other hand, the lie and the liar are much disparaged. The Bible explicitly warns against lying: "You shall not bear false witness" (Exodus 20:13); "Keep far from a false matter" (Exodus 23:7); and "Neither shall you deal falsely nor lie to one another" (Leviticus 19:11). Also, witness this observation from the Jewish Talmud: "Such is the punishment of the liar—even if he tells the truth he is not believed" (Sanhedrin 89b). Likewise, the Greek philosophers found virtue in truth. Plato observed: "It is truth which you cannot contradict" *(Symposium,* 201).

Theologians, philosophers, and jurists have emphasized the need for the truth to protect the very foundations of the social order. For instance, in the fifth century, Augustine, the church father, stated that truthfulness was necessary because: "When regard for truth has broken down or even slightly weakened, all things remain doubtful."[22] Augustine did agree that some lies were much worse, notably those stated in the name of religion, while some might be pardonable, such as those that harm no one and save someone from a serious injury.[23] In the Middle Ages, the thirteenth-century theologian Thomas Aquinas in his great work on theology described mischievous or malicious lies as mortal sins, though he excepted two other types—lies that were helpful and those told in jest.[24] In the eighteenth century, the German philosopher Immanuel Kant took an absolutist position against all lies, claiming that all should be prohibited, regardless of their nature. He claimed truth is an "unconditional duty which holds in all circumstances" and should be limited by "no expediency," no matter how great the disadvantage to oneself or another. Why should truth be so important? According to Kant, lies always harm humanity in general, even if they do not wrong any particular person. The reason? The lie "vitiates the source of law" and destroys the human dignity of the liar.[25]

Some thinkers try to propose conditions under which lying is acceptable. Hugo Grotius, a seventeenth-century Dutch scholar, suggested that a falsehood becomes a lie and should be forbidden only if it prevents someone who deserves it from hearing the truth.[26] Another school of thought advanced by the casuist thinkers permits a person to use a mental reservation to make a misleading statement true. The idea here is that a speaker can't be held responsible if someone else misinterprets his statement. For instance, if you say, "I didn't do it," and then did, but think to yourself "I didn't do it when you said I did," that would no longer be a lie. Still other thinkers question the premise that every untruth is morally wrong, suggesting that if a deception is designed to benefit the person deceived, it may as a matter of sense sometimes be right, an approach taken by the nineteenth-century English philosopher Henry Sidgwick.[27]

Because of this quibbling about the value of truth and the morality of lying, religious leaders, philosophers, and others have fried to come up with guidelines about what is appropriate. A list of admonitions is suggested by religious leader Mark Dratch, who proposes some of the following:

> "Absolute veracity is essential in judicial proceedings .
>   "Lying is forbidden when it results in harm to another
> . .
>   "One may deviate from the truth for the sake of peace as well as for other ethical imperatives such as humility, modesty, and sensitivity . . . Even in those cases in which mendacity is permitted, habitual falsehood is forbidden . . .
>   "The falsehood injunction proscribes more than the articulation of untrue statements. It includes any communication or impression of false ideas—articulated and unarticulated—through action and through inaction, in speech and in print . .
>   "In those cases where lying is permitted, ambiguity is to be preferred over an outright falsehood. It is preferable to make an equivocal statement that is truthful in its intended version but that may be misinterpreted by the listener."[28]

If such moral and ethical guidelines do not keep people in line, there is always the inbred belief or fear that "truth will out."[29] Perhaps the more modern version of this concern is the oft-quoted phrase "What goes around comes around."

The original stricture may speak from a moral force urging good behavior (and presumably honesty) to get good behavior (and presumably honesty) in return. But the modern version also reflects the pragmatism of the modern world. "Don't do it if it's wrong, because if you do, someone may do the same thing to you." The change is subtle, but it reflects the decline in the hold of traditional moral and ethical thinking about controlling behavior and marks the rise of a more secular, pragmatic, results-oriented thinking.

Yet, despite the potential danger of the lie being found out or coming back to harm us, we lie, and the texture of lying is woven into everyday life, because we make unconscious—maybe even conscious—cost-benefit analyses of lying in a situation, weighing the risks of being found out and the losses of not lying against the potential gains.

Ann Landers once asked her readers to send in their ideas of the "third biggest lie." The two biggest that she suggested were: "I'm from the government and I'm here to help you," and "The check is in the mail." She was deluged with mail. One of her columns was devoted to the suggestions, echoing the many examples I heard as I asked people about the lies they encountered. The table on the following page shows some of them, most of which have a familiar ring.

It's as if people lie and expect lies to the point that common falsehoods are so common they are no longer considered lies. Should this be? In doing my interviews, I found that some people were quite bothered by this, though they experienced or sometimes did it themselves. "Just why do we have to lie?" some of them were asking, even as they saw lying as a common reality.

How much of a reality? According to a recent study reported by Daniel Goleman, the average adult lies—or admits to doing so—thirteen times a week.[31] According to Arthur Goldberg, a professor of psychiatry at Rush Medical College in Chicago, "Lying is as much a part of normal growth and development as telling the truth."[32] Psychologists have identified key areas that motivate people to lie, such as to gain a sense of independence from the control or intrusiveness of others; to gain power and control; to repress or deny a source of conflict or unpleasantness; and to express a wish or increase self-esteem, say, by embroidering the truth or embellishing achievements to appear more "sought after, accomplished, or admirable."[33]

Some authors even suggest we live in a culture where lies have been institutionalized and are used routinely by our leaders. For instance, in a thoughtful article on "The Culture of Lying" in *The New Republic,* Mark Hosenball uses examples from the

Common Lies People Encounter

Social lies

"Five pounds is nothing on a person with your height."

"It's delicious, but I can't eat another bite."

"Your hair looks just fine."

"You made it yourself? I never would have guessed."

"So glad you dropped by. I wasn't doing a thing."

"You don't look a day over forty."

"The baby is just beautiful."

"You can tell me. I won't breathe a word to a soul."

"Having a great time. Wish you were here."

Sales lies

"It's a good thing you came in today. We have only two more in stock."

"The river never gets high enough to flood this property."

"You don't need it in writing. You have my personal guarantee."

"This is a very safe building. No way will you ever be burglarized."

"This car is like brand new."

Man-woman lies

"Sorry, dear, not tonight. I have a headache."

"Of course I will respect you in the morning."

"You have nothing to worry about, honey. I've had a vasectomy."

"Put the map away. I know exactly how to get there."

Parent-child lies

"Go ahead and tell me. I promise I won't get mad."

"The puppy won't be any trouble, Mom. I promise to take care of it myself."

"Our children never caused us a minute's trouble."

"I've finished my homework."

"Dad, I need to move out of the dorm into an apartment of my own so I can have some peace and quiet when I study."

Work lies

"Sorry, the work isn't ready. The computer broke down."

"The new ownership won't affect you. The company will remain the same."

"I gave at the office."

Doctor-patient lies

"It's nothing to worry about—just a cold sore."

"The doctor will call you right back."

Lies to officials

"But, officer, I only had two beers."

Self-lies

"I'm a social drinker, and I can quit any time I want to."

All-purpose lies

"I did it. I didn't do it. I can't remember."

"I'll do it in a minute."30

Irangate scandals to illustrate four types of lies—the outrageous lie, repeated frequently and vehemently until others believe it; the crafty lie, which creates a fog of confusing statements and evasions; the patriotic lie, which uses a sincere conviction as justification for the lie; and the muddled lie, in which perpetrators maintain their stories are confused rather than false 34

The motivation to lie can be extremely powerful, whether we use a lie as a sword to go after something or as a shield to protect ourselves. As psychologist Beverly Palmer of California State University put it in a *USA Today* interview: We commonly use lying to protect ourselves "from the other person's angry or hurt feelings. We lie when we feel insecure, scared, or we're trying to escape consequences of our actions."[35] But then, we run into the consequences of lying—the moral taboos, the threats to relationships and community, and the possible damages to ourselves if caught.

It was this central paradox that guided me as I explored this subject and asked questions in my interviews. When did people lie, and why? When and why did others lie to them? How did they feel about lying? What did they do to deal with it? When did they feel the lie was justified? What did they do if they thought someone was lying to them? Bring it out in the open? Let it lie? Pursue other strategies? How could they tell if someone was lying?

In these interviews, I spoke to a representative sampling of men and women who could be considered successful business and professional people, part of the mainstream. I spoke to seven women and seven men in formal interviews, and another two dozen or so informally in everyday conversations.

I also spoke with experts—psychologists and therapists who have encountered and dealt with lying in their own practice; specialists on male-female relationships, often a prime area for lying; and two business consultants working with corporations and small businesses.

The following chapters describe the results of these explorations, as well as my own reflections and reactions to the central paradox of how and why we lie in everyday life.

CHAPTER 2

Why the Lie?

The Reasons &
Justifications for Lying

*J*UST ABOUT ANY SITUATION WHERE PEOPLE INTERACT holds the potential for lying. And even when alone, people can lie to themselves. It's no wonder that most people I spoke with about lying agreed that it is at least somewhat common and comes in many forms—everything from the outright fabrication to the evasive half-truth, concealment, or unintended promise.

What is common? The people I spoke to reported that others lied to them about once or twice a week, and they averaged about one or two lies each week themselves—though most were "white lies" committed to save people's feelings and smooth over social relations.

There are so many types of lies that turn up in so many different situations and are told for so many reasons that it can be hard to determine whether a statement really is a lie. Was it intended as a lie? Was it perceived as a lie? Did it feel like a lie?

Types of Lies

Lies can be like soup—they come in a variety of packages with different contents, sizes, and prices. Some are much bigger and richer than others; some smaller and less expensive, and for that reason probably more popular and common. In turn, people have different preferences, regardless of size or price, and some people may have different ways of defining what belongs in the category (i.e., At what point does changing the ingredients make it a broth or a stew?).

The type of lying most clearly perceived as lying—and which is usually thought of as worse than any other type—is the outright fabrication of something presented as true or fact. You know it's three o'clock, but he says two. It's the overt lie or lie of commission.

Such a lie differs from the mistake, for the person *knows* what he is presenting as true is not; he is directly seeking to deceive—the essence of the lie.

But then, that's also the least common type of lying. What seem to be more common are the half-truths, which contain some but not all of the true information, or present what's true in a misleading way; the omissions or concealments, which leave out something important and relevant; and the commitments and promises made that one doesn't intend to keep. Then, too, these statements need not be verbal; they can be made with gestures and nods, even silences can be taken to be an assent or a disagreement with something said.

I've tried to define lying broadly to encompass these different views; but these varying viewpoints still can lead to different ideas about why people lie and when lying is appropriate.

For example, take concealing. It could be considered a lie when the information covered up or not said is something one would be expected to say, such as the husband concealing his mistress. He doesn't tell his wife he has a mistress, because she doesn't ask, so he is not misstating the truth—he is just not telling it. In such a case, not telling would become a lie, because the understanding with his wife is that he will not do this. So concealing a failure to honor an agreement becomes the lie. Similarly, only a partial truth when the whole truth would give the full picture could be a lie, too. An example: When a person says, "I'll have to cancel the appointment because my car is in the shop," and the real truth is that he decided to do something else instead and took the car to the shop because he no longer needed it to make his appointment.

There were other people who thought that concealment for a good purpose wasn't really a lie, such as withholding an unfavorable bit of news from someone with a bad heart. "I don't think that's lying, if you're assessing what you can safely say and are looking out for someone's welfare," another woman told me. There were others who disagreed. Sure, it was a lie to conceal for a good purpose; though it was one of those white and beneficial lies. Then again there were still others who questioned the virtue of such concealments, claiming it was better to know the truth.

As one man put it: "For me, withholding information would be lying if you knew that not withholding it would make a difference in your relationship or transaction or you used it to influence the outcome. Or if you knew this was important information you should reveal. Then I would consider it a form of lying."

Similarly, commitments can be fuzzy. While some people might not consider not keeping a promise or commitment a type of lie—"It's just a lack of integrity," as one man said—others see it as a lie if the promise or commitment is made without the intention of keeping it. Or, as one man put it, "If someone consciously intends to not be there, and they say they're going to be there, that's a lie to me." Another woman made this fine distinction: "If you don't intend to do it at the time you make the agreement, that feels like lying. But if you have the intention to do it but then you don't do it, then I think it's just not keeping agreements and having a lack of integrity." If the reason for not doing it is error or forgetfulness, that's just a "mistake," as one man said. Roger, a college philosophy teacher, made this distinction:

II Breaking an agreement or lying are two separate things. An agreement is something that's going to happen in the future, and you may or may not be able to keep your agreements, based on what occurs. So there might be contingencies that prevent you from keeping an agreement, such as one time when I made an agreement to substitute-teach for a friend, and it was raining, and I couldn't get there because it was so slow on the freeways. So I got there late. But it was beyond my control to get there on time to keep the agreement, so there was no lie. And if I had forgotten, that wouldn't be a lie either. It would show a lack of integrity, but it wouldn't be a lie.

However, a lie might be involved if one makes an agreement in bad faith. For instance, there was a man who was living upstairs from me who borrowed $10 to fix his car. He promised to pay me back. But he lied, because there was nothing wrong with his car; he was just out of gas. And then he didn't keep his promise to pay me, either. He promised that he was going to take the money to get his car going and then he was going to get his paycheck. As I found out later, he didn't have a job then. So that was a lie, too, because he was making an agreement that he knew he couldn't keep. He was making the agreement to get some kind of benefit for himself, but he had no intention of ever keeping the agreement. And that's a lie.

Also the whole area of self-presentation and image-making seems to be fertile ground for debating whether the presentation of the image is a lie or not. Again, the key factor seems to be the individual's intent in making the presentation and whether he is leaving out information that would be considered important or relevant or whether he is adding information that might mislead. The notion of affirming or presenting oneself in a positive light seems fine, though this shades over into exaggeration and bragging. But more about this in a later chapter.

As Roger, the philosophy teacher, expressed this paradox in defining this sort of lie:

0   I don't consider presenting the truth in a favorable perspective to be lying. Say you're applying for a position, and there's a two-year gap between your graduate school and your first teaching job, because you had a difficult time finding yourself. I don't consider it lying not to put down the details, because that's personal information and it could directly interfere with your getting a job which you can do. So as long as you can do the job, I think it's appropriate to present the information on your résumé to your best advantage.

Roger gave an example of a man he knew who did this.

I   He was a professor who was applying for a job at a school where I was teaching. He did not have his Ph.D. so on his vita he simply did not list his degrees. He was interviewed, and the committee liked him, so he got the position. After he was in the position for a few years, a committee came around to verify his credentials, and they found out he didn't have his Ph.D., though he had been doing a good job. Eventually he was fired for misrepresenting himself. That's the case where I'd consider it dishonest to misrepresent oneself in that way, because letting people assume that you have a Ph.D. when you do not, to gain an advantage, is a case of deliberately withholding certain critical information you should disclose. So that's a case of telling a lie through falsely presenting the self.

In other cases, this emphasis on the positive and withholding of the negative seemed fine. It was part of the philosophy of affirming the self or making others feel good by accentuating the positive. So it wasn't a lie. If it was, it was one of those benevolent white lies, and therefore fine.

For example, Roger explained:

I   When you go for an interview, certainly you don't declare all of your frailties. You try to put yourself forward in the best possible light. Or when you go out on a date, you don't go into the details of your sexual behavior until you really know the person. In my case, I do want to share every aspect of my life with another person that I'm intimate with. But not all at one time or in the beginning. So I don't consider that I'm misrepresenting myself when I don't tell all in the beginning.

It's the same way when you're trying to impress someone, say at a mixer. In a certain way, you're presenting an aspect of you that's not the total you, but I don't consider that lying. For that's the crucial difference—the difference between presenting yourself in a positive light and deliberately withholding some information that one would normally expect to be there.

Likewise, for some people the idea of couching a critical evaluation in a positive light is not a lie, either. For example, while purists might consider anything less than the complete truth to be lying, albeit for the best of intentions, the philosophy teacher quoted above described this positive approach to framing or shaping reality in this light:

I   I don't consider presenting the facts in a favorable perspective to be lying. For instance, if someone asked me: "How do you like my dress?" or something like that, I think

I can express the fact that I don't think it is the best or that
it doesn't bring out the best in a person and still make the
person feel affirmed. In other words, I'm presenting a
perspective on the situation. It may be a favored perspective on the situation, but it's still an interpretation of events
. . . I'm finding something positive to say; I'm not trying to
put the negative in some positive context. But that's not
lying, because I don't see lying and the truth as direct
opposites, so that whenever you don't tell the full truth,
that doesn't mean you're automatically lying, as if these
are direct contraries. Rather, lying involves deliberately
trying to mislead or deceive someone. But just putting
things in a positive light doesn't do that.

In short, lies can run the gamut from the outright, overt misstatement of the truth to those other half-truths, concealments, and
broken promises that some people think of as lies only in some
circumstances. In any case, if someone considers something to be a
lie, whether he does it or someone else does it to him, then so be it—
I have viewed it as a lie for the purposes of this book. The essence of
the lie is the conscious intent to deceive, no matter what forms that
deceit takes.

The Reasons for Lying

When I interviewed people, some of the same reasons kept coming
up for both the women and men as to when they lied or someone
lied to them. The most popular reason—especially for the women—
was to spare someone's feelings or make someone feel better, the
altruistic side of lying.

Most other reasons revolved around gaining an advantage or
improving one's appearance, such as getting out of some activity or
event, appearing more skilled or knowledgeable, improving one's
reputation, hiding a mistake, covering up something, keeping a
secret, or gaining a financial advantage or position in business. In
addition, another reason for lying was revenge or jealousy.

Beyond these situational reasons are deeper motives for lying.
At its roots—and certainly this is why the tool of lying and deceit
has been programmed into us—lying is a defense mechanism
designed to protect the individual or others he chooses to protect.
As Mark, a business consultant, put it forcefully, we lie for survival. As he said:

0   What human beings do is primarily for survival, and
      survival includes looking good, being right, justifying

ourselves, dominating the situation. That is, if we are right, we survive. So we do everything to survive. So we will lie, cheat, steal, all in the name of our own survival. And so we always have some way to justify the lie. It may not work—I don't think it does in the long run. But lying is absolutely congruent with survival. And to survive, we can justify anything—including cheating on our wives and our husbands, cheating on our taxes, whatever. We're seeking the short-term gain and justifying it to ourselves. Because the lie is about survival—lying for our own advantage to survive.

In turn, this use of lying as a defense mechanism may lead to lying to the self and to others to avoid facing an unpleasant reality. A psychotherapist I spoke to, Robert Young, a practitioner for the Progress Foundation, a private, nonprofit organization working with mentally ill patients, explained:

Sometimes as a defense, people may deny what is true or even conjure up images of multiple personalities, because they so need to defend against the truth as to provide a reality they can live with. So they have to lie to themselves and other people.

For example, a classic case is the woman who has experienced sexual molestation or abuse. Some women who have been abused cannot really consider that it is true. So they might say, no, it never happened, or it was a dream, or people are lying about it.

Then there are other sorts of lies that in their more extreme form reflect personality or character disorders, such as the narcissistic personality disorder, where a person has such grandiose thoughts of himself as important, valuable, or good that his ideas become pathological.

What are the major factors that trigger such uses of the lie? Common triggers are stress, attack, or risk. As Stephen, a writer, commented:

Generally, I would say I've lied to others when I have felt under stress or maybe under attack for some reason. Either there's some sort of stress occurring in my life or in my relationship with someone. So the lie is a way to protect myself or gain an advantage somehow . . . And then I found I have lied when I felt at risk in some way, either emotionally or physically, though emotionally mostly. For example, suppose the woman I'm with asks me a question about herself or asks for my opinion on something, and I think she's expecting or wants a certain answer, but my answer isn't that. I might lie to smooth things over, such as saying "I love you," or "I agree with you," when I'm not feeling that emotion or that opinion at the time.

As psychologist Robert Young pointed out, such feelings of stress or attack can help the person justify the lie. As he explained:

Stress tends to make lying less of a sin. Stress tends to make it more allowable to lie. Say if you have to get something done by a deadline, and the boss asks, are you going to have it done? You may know you are not going to have it done. So you may say, yes, you'll finish it, just to get him off your back, and hope that maybe it will get done after all. So stress in general can tend to make people be less truthful.

Under stress, people may look to all sorts of excuses to justify the lie. As Young commented:

I think drugs and alcohol are a bit of a fad excuse now for excusing yourself for your own personal behavior. "It wasn't me, it was my substance abuse." So these substances can be used to excuse lies as well as other kinds of behavior, particularly since the general population is now coming to see alcoholism as a disease, and hence beyond one's ability to control. This disease theory may not be true. But whether it is or not, people use the excuse of drugs or alcohol to say "I couldn't stop myself," Or "I couldn't control myself," Or "I didn't mean to do it," "It's not my fault, I was drunk," or "I was on drugs."

In turn, this stress theory of lying suggests that people subjected to economic stress—people earning less money—might be more likely to lie, and I asked Young about this. I pointed out that the successful professional and business people I interviewed had emphasized their own generally high ethical standards and that my transcriber, earning much less money and living in a small apartment near the ocean in San Francisco had commented on this cynically: "It's nice that somebody in such a secure financial position can afford to be so honest. But when you have to keep it together financially, you have to think of your own survival. Sometimes you have to lie to survive."

Is this true? Was this real difference in the propensity to lie based on income? I didn't choose to study this difference in this book, but certainly, my own experience and what I have read suggest this.

While economic insecurity can add fuel to the fires of fear that lead to lying, people can be insecure for all sorts of reasons that lead to lying. That was a theme I heard repeated again and again when I asked why people lie. Judith Briles, who has studied the ethics of women and men in the corporate world in her two books—Women *to Women: From Sabotage to Support* and *The Confidence* Factor—observed in an interview:

> Often people feel drawn to lying and justified in doing it because they feel they aren't getting their worth recognized. They aren't getting their due. They have not been honored. They haven't been credited for something . . . Something has happened to make them feel diminished, insecure. For the act of lying is birthed out of fear. It's birthed out of insecurity. It's birthed out of low confidence. Sometimes you can have jealousy and other things thrown in as well, but that's the bottom line—insecurity and fear.

Still another common reason, born out of insecurity, was a desire for increased self-esteem. As Frances, a computer-systems supervisor in a large manufacturing company, put it:

> II   I've run into lying a lot with people seeking a job or a better position. They don't feel good enough about themselves to tell the truth. So they're compensating for a lack of security and self-esteem. They have to puff themselves up to make themselves look better . . . And we've all seen this with people in the public eye as well. For instance, some candidates, such as Teddy Kennedy, have lied about their undergraduate work. And there was one woman here in San Francisco, running for supervisor, who said she had done certain things on her résumé when she had not. So that's a big one, I think, self-esteem.

Robert Young, the psychotherapist, backed up this low self-esteem factor from his own practice. He saw many people with eroded confidence engaging in lies to deny their sense of failure to themselves, create a protective fantasy that things would really be fine, or try to maintain a good face for others. As Young observed:

> Society has become so dynamic and changing today that it tends to disrupt people's confidence, such as when a person loses a job and can't find another. A concrete example might be the guy who's trained as a tool-and-die maker. He gets out of tool-and-die—making school, but then he's out of a job in five years, and a lot of his sense of self-worth is shattered because now he's no longer able to provide for his family. He's out of a job, or maybe he's working at a low-income job, such as the 7-Eleven at $3.50 an hour . . . . The person has been trained with certain skills for a skilled job and suddenly has nowhere to use them. So his self-confidence is eroded, which can happen to anyone who suddenly encounters closed doors and feels his sense of self undermined . . . .
>
> And then, as a result of this lack of self-confidence, the person mostly wants to deny. So lying becomes a way of covering up, of trying to maintain a facade, or of saying to himself, it's not so bad, it will get better, I'll get another job doing this, when in fact, there are no jobs. The lie becomes a way to protect against the lack of self-worth and confidence the person feels.

A desire not to admit or to hide something could lead to lies to oneself—to avoid facing something unpleasant; or lies to others— to avoid feeling shame.

For example, Raphael, a counselor and healer, encountered many people lying to him, both clients and associates, because they were afraid to be direct and revealing.

> I think people often are not direct and open about what's happening, because they may not want to admit to something to someone else. Or they may not want to look at something in themselves.
>
> For example, that happened with some of the people I worked for who decided our working arrangement wasn't working out. They were in authority, and they could use their power to make it seem like I wasn't

doing things the way they wanted. But the approaches I was using were working, and I wanted them to look at their own issues and reasons. But they said no, trying to make me seem in the wrong, because they didn't want to see what was going on in themselves.

Raphael also encountered the concealing and hiding.

| It happens when you don't want people to know something about you which may affect how these people treat you or think about you. So you say things that aren't true or leave things out—lies of commission or lies of omission. But they can be used for the same reason—to try to hide something. For example, you are asked something directly: you say no or you don't know. It can be an easy way of getting off the hook or keeping someone out, instead of maybe being more direct and saying "mind your own business." I know I've used that sometimes; and others have used it on me. I think we all sometimes have things we want to hide, and lying, or maybe more accurately, concealing, can be a way to do this.

Likewise, Stan, a usually honest high-school teacher, used lies to hide a smoking habit from his wife. He suspected that she knew, because there was the smell of smoke everywhere—though she never said anything—because it would be too stressful to deal with the subject.

Another type of lie, born of insecurity, is the passive-aggressive style of lying, described as a common dynamic in lying by one of the therapists I spoke with, Sylvia Mills, a psychotherapist in private practice who deals with primarily professional and business clients. In this case, the person feels insecure and so hangs back from being assertive and saying what he or she really wants. Instead, he or she says something, agrees to something, or goes along with something he or she really doesn't want, and so, in effect, lives a lie. That failure to be authentic can lead to anger and resentment, which can be expressed through open hostility, distancing in relationships, or covert behavior, such as back-stabbing or sabotage. Mills explained the process, illustrating it with an experience with two friends.

| Basically, what happens with the passive-aggressive person, is he or she seems very agreeable. It's like he or she is Mr. Nice Guy, so nice and ready to do things

your way. But all the time they're agreeing, they are burning up with resentment, because they are "giving in" and not doing what they want to do.

For example, if I'm a passive-aggressive person, which I'm not, I might agree to go to a movie with you, saying: "Okay, I'll go to the movie you want to see," but I'll sit through that movie thinking: "I don't want to sit through this movie. I want to go to the other movie." And meanwhile, I'll be angry or hating you, because I've gone to your choice of a movie instead of speaking up for myself.

Finally, after numerous occasions of giving in, the resentment is voiced. These angry feelings are typically directed at the other person for being "inconsiderate." It's hard for Mr. or Mrs. Nice Guy to take responsibility for their own passivity—and so much easier to project out all the responsibility and blame.

The irony of all this is that the other person is usually feeling quite warm toward their "considerate" partner. Thus it's a rude shock to discover the partner has been lying about his or her real feelings.

How does this happen? I wondered, and Mills explained:

In one case, the woman—I'll call her Judy—was friends with another woman, Sally, whom she thought was a real friend. And then one day, when the two of them were in a group of about half a dozen people, Sally suddenly announced that she really didn't like something that Judy did. She thought Judy was bossy and controlling, that Judy always wanted to do things her way, and so she had gone along with Judy in the past. But now, she griped about how she resented that.

And Judy was shocked because she had known Sally for three years, and Sally never complained about anything.

Now Sally was saying she had felt this way for three years. To make matters worse, she was making this accusation in a very public group with Judy's friends. Judy was really furious and disgusted. She felt her relationship with Sally for over three years had been based on trust.

They had both shared so much of their lives with each other. Now in this very public way, Judy suddenly felt that Sally had come out and negated that trust. So that ended the relationship, since Judy now

realized the lie Sally had been hiding for all these
years; her feelings of trust were shattered.

Another big reason for lying, which can also be traced to fears
and insecurity, is the desire to avoid embarrassment or save face or
to make oneself look better.

Don, a fifty-something engineer, for example, felt embarrassed
telling the store owner his real reason for getting a dog whistle.
When the owner asked whether he had a dog, he quietly fibbed and
said he did.

"But the real reason," Don told me, "is that I wanted to get this
whistle to annoy this dog next door to get him to stop barking. I
wanted to train him so that every time he barked, he would hear this
unpleasant whistle, and that might get him to stop. But then, I
thought it might not be proper to use the whistle in this way. You're
supposed to use it to get the dog's attention so you can train it. But
this isn't what I was doing, and maybe if I started explaining my real
reasons, the owner might think I might want to blow the whistle to
have the dog bark more so it would bother other people, and then we
could all get together to get rid of the dog."

A few days later Don encountered a case of someone lying to
make himself look good. It was one of those name-dropping
situations, where Don and a girlfriend had gone to a party and
had sat with a man who was telling stories about his successful
exploits in building companies and making high-yield invest-
ments. He also described exciting international adventures where
he had eluded some potential robbers or killers, presumably after
some of his expensive belongings or his money. People had listened in rapt fascination.

But when Don and his girlfriend drove the man home and Don
asked him more detailed and pointed questions, it soon became
apparent that some of his stories could not have happened.
"Things just didn't jibe right or hang together," Don said, "so we
concluded he must be a pathological liar. He was just trying to
make himself look good or more important. And he could do
that—he could say anything he wanted to impress—because no
people bothered to check out or question his story, or maybe
didn't know enough to do so. So that's what he was doing—
building himself up to impress everyone with what a great guy he
was."

Another reason for lying is to gain power—a reason often used
for lies in business to gain an advantage or in conflicts of lovers and
spouses, usually by the woman, because she has less power.

For instance, as Dee, a real-estate investor, observed: "If people lie to me, I would lie back to them if I feel that it's necessary to be on a more equal footing with them. As I see it, the lie is a way of gaining power in a situation. So in that case I would use it if someone isn't going to be straight or fair with me. It's like my way of evening out the deck if someone else is trying to play with the cards."

Then there are lies of convenience. It's just easier to lie than to raise issues that might otherwise be discussed; easier to lie than to have to give explanations; easier to lie than to have to deal with feelings or perhaps hurt someone's feelings by telling the truth.

Lies can also be used to get someone to do something or to get out of doing something oneself. Roger, the philosophy teacher, described how one of his colleagues did this, and ironically, this was a professor of ethics who used promises he didn't keep to gain an advantage. As Roger told me:

I   This teacher, Jack, got a one-year sabbatical from his university for a year of study at a big eastern university in some ethics program, and so he had to move there. Well, he knew a graduate student who had a truck. So Jack promised this student that "You move me to Harvard with your truck, and I'll set up interviews with all of these teachers I know there to help you get into Harvard."

The student brought his truck around, loaded up Jack's furniture, and drove him from this school in the South all the way to Massachusetts—a distance of almost a thousand miles.

But then, a few months later, when the student returned to Massachusetts, wanting to set up the interviews, Jack had totally forgotten about his promises. "What promise?" he said. "I didn't promise you anything."

So the graduate student didn't get his interviews and didn't get in, and he was totally furious, because Jack reneged on what he said he was going to do. Maybe the student wouldn't have gotten in anyway. But the point is that Jack used the student to get what he wanted. And then, after he was moved to Harvard, and didn't need the student anymore, he just reneged.

Then there are the lies that hurt or wound others. Often they are born of jealousy or revenge. If true hurtful evidence isn't available, sometimes someone will make up something.

Don, the engineer, described what happened when he and a former lover were having a fight:

> She said some very insulting things to me—making up insults to hurl against me. She claimed I couldn't do this, couldn't do that, said I didn't have the feelings I said I had, that sort of thing. And then she said I didn't do things that I did.
>
> I knew the things she was saying weren't true, and I don't know whether she had spaced out and literally forgot things that had happened, or was making things up, just to have things to throw at me. I suspect the latter, and when I tried to confront her, to point out how these things weren't true, she replied she was just joking. But I don't think she was. She clearly wasn't saying things in a joking way. I felt she was saying them to put me down, and was trying to make me think she thought these things about me, whether true or not. So she was just trying to get me, I think, by making up lies.

Also, revenge can be an underlying motivation, which is what happened to Reba, a speaker on inspirational themes.

By mistake, she disclosed information about a former coach and trainer, and he was very angry about it, so angry that that ended their teacher-student relationship, and he barely spoke to her for years. But besides that, he did even more, as Reba later found out.

> I learned about it from my boyfriend. The man was spreading stories about me, claiming I was unreliable, that I wasn't as good and competent as I presented myself, things like that. And then, when I confronted him about it, he told me: "Well now you know how I felt, because you disclosed something I had told you in confidence about me."
>
> Well, until then I never realized I had let anything slip before—he had never told me, just acted odd and distant. And then he further retaliated by telling false stories about me. I feel like he should have told me what was bothering him in the first place, because I realized when I spoke to a couple of friends about this that I could have inappropriately disclosed things. But then, I don't think that justifies what he did against me—I had just made a mistake, but he was out to actually hurt me, to get back at me for revenge.

While most reasons for lying reflect the dark side of lying, there are also good reasons for some lies. Some are designed to help and protect someone else and are referred to as "white lies," although the term also refers to the trivial lies used about things of small importance and little consequence. As Stan, the teacher, explained:

I   There were a couple of times that I lied to my wife, but this was to help her.
       What happened was that she was very ill with cancer, and she was on chemical treatment for a year. I had to continually reassure her that she was doing fine, that she was getting better, although for a while it didn't look that way. But I felt I was helping her, at least to brighten her spirits, even if she couldn't be cured. But then, eventually, she did beat it, and it could be that maybe the lie helped. So I think sometimes it is possible to help someone by lying, and then I think it's okay to lie.

Stan similarly used lies from time to time to encourage and motivate his students. Again he felt lying was justified, because it was done to help. As he told me:

11   I think it's okay to lie when it's making people feel okay about themselves or encouraging them to do something. And I've done this with my students. For instance, a kid comes up and asks me: "Am I really flunking?" and the kid probably is flunking now. However, the kid by law is going to be in my class until June, with several months to go. So if I was to tell him he is flunking, I'd probably never see him again. So instead, I would tell him, well, maybe if you really buckle down and start coming and make up this work, maybe you'll pass.
       In a way it's a lie, because probably the student is not going to do what he needs to do to pass, and I suspect the student feels he can't pass anyway. But I think it's a worthwhile lie because it helps and encourages him a little.

Then, of course, there are the self-lies committed to protect and build up the self to the self. Such lies can start off as deceptions to others, but as the person tells them again and again, they can turn into deceptions to the self.

Psychotherapist Robert Young explained how people might come to believe their own lies.

I   When someone creates a fantasy to impress people, that could be an example of narcissism. And sometimes they might believe it themselves, sometimes not; or the fantasy could be a blending of both.

And often what happens is that the story they tell can grow into them, so they come to believe it more and more as time goes on. Just the process of telling and retelling can help them believe, so after a while, truth and fantasy become so artfully blended or they have repeated the imagined claim so often that they think it is true.

Moreover, as Young suggested, if the fantasies and deceptions become great enough, the syndrome isn't just narcissism. The clinical term for what is occurring is grandiosity, which often appears in manic-depressives when they are in the manic phase, and often is accompanied or eased by alcohol or drugs that help to support the fantasy.

Why would lies and deceptions go so far as to turn into a psychiatrically identified syndrome of mental illness?

"Because then," Young explained, "the narcissistic or grandiose lie has become a defense against a more serious inner turmoil, such as a defense against either depression, which is most probable, or some other sort of trauma. The lie becomes that much greater, because it is a defense against more serious problems."

Even if such self-lies don't go so far as to become forms of illnesses, they can still be used as a psychological defense against reality.

This is what happened when Blanche's husband lost his job. He was an engineer who lost his job in the defense industry and couldn't readily find another. So Blanche, as an act of love, not because she needed him, hired him to work in her own start-up business. He began to think he was important to the company, though he wasn't; instead he was inefficient and ineffective in his managerial duties, though he didn't want to admit this when Blanche tried to point it out.

"Now, that's a good example of denial to escape facing reality," Young told me. "These kind of false build-ups of self are always a kind of defense against reality. After all, if her husband was to really see himself as he is, he would have to face the fact that he is a failure, and then, who knows what could happen?"

Then, too, some lies may be used to help the social good—a Trojan horse sort of lie designed to gain a strategic advantage in a conflict, or the patriotic or nationalistic lie designed to cover up something in the name of national security. Plus, a lie might be used to save a life other than one's own, as in the classic "he-went-thataway" ploy used to protect someone from being hurt by another. As Young observed:

I   Classically, the philosophers and moralists have said, "Don't lie." Kant said that one should never lie.
     But then there's the classic counterargument show-ing there are times when the lie can be appropriate.
     For instance, what if a man comes running through your room and says, "There's a murderer chasing me and he has a gun in his hand?" And then, after the man runs off, the murderer comes in, saying: "Where did that guy go?" If you tell the truth, you might be responsible for the man's death, whereas a lie might save him. So there can be times when lies are appropriate. This may be an exaggerated example, but there are times.

Then there is the lie, which also may be benign, that allows us to step into another reality for a while by creating not just a better image but another persona for the self. It is a way, as the philosopher Elizabeth Kamarck Minnich describes it, of giving us "an almost magical sense of our own power and freedom," and as such it is "like imagination, like creativity, like play." It is a way of lying "for fun," to show that one is "not bound by the facts of the matter."[2]

Raphael, the healer and counselor, gave a good example of this when he described how he had literally created a new char-acter for himself when he went to a local restaurant. As he de-scribed it, it was an exaggerated, eccentric, free-spirited, looser, freewheeling, and entertaining image of his usual self.

II   I can be whoever I want to be. It's kind of fun. I can step into this other role and be light-spirited. If I'm really in a magical mood, I can say some nice things. Or I can wear something unique and different. Sometimes I wear black. Sometimes a unique hat. Sometimes some earrings, or other touches. It's just interesting to create this public versus my private person. I think there's something exhibitionistic about what I'm doing. And it's fun.

Justifying the Lie

Ironically, people generally say they don't like to lie, sometimes feel guilty or bad about lying, dislike it or even feel angry and betrayed when others lie to them. Yet they commonly feel their own lies are justified or appropriate. In fact, people sometimes feel proud of certain lies.

This sense of justification is due to what psychologists call "homeostasis"—achieving a sense of psychological balance so that one can feel good or comfortable about however one has acted.

When I spoke with psychotherapist Robert Young, he explained justifying the lie this way:

| Lying is fundamentally wrong. Everyone would generally acknowledge that. Though many people have a relativistic ethic, making it okay to lie to certain groups of people or under certain circumstances. For example, it's okay to lie to an enemy like the Iranians. It's okay to lie to someone who has lied to you before. It's okay to lie to ruin someone's reputation, because that person has already done something to do me in and therefore deserves it. And then we define some lies as okay, because they are done to help people.

In other words, lies are normally justified. There's always some hidden agenda in the lie, some good reason or bad reason that justifies the lie. And the underlying dynamic behind this is the psychological process known as homeostasis, which is a way of keeping balance. We use justification to not be out of balance. So if you have a good reason to lie you'll feel much healthier and calmer about yourself.

In some cases, an outside observer wouldn't agree with that reason. He may think it's a bad reason. But the person engaging in the lie will think it's a good reason; he'll feel it is justified; it's his way of staying in balance, in homeostasis with himself.

Otherwise, without doing this, the individual might feel some internal or intrapsychic dissonance, resulting in feelings of anxiety or paranoia. So people will come up with reasons so they feel comfortable about what they do.

As Young pointed out, some of the reasons might seem to be valid justifications to someone else. For instance, a sleazy salesperson might not tell a customer that the brakes on the car he was buying were bad because the salesman might tell himself: "If the customer didn't bother to check, he's stupid and deserves what he gets." Or taking an example on a wider scale—a national leader might justify a lie in the interests of national security, such as "I lied to the Iranians to try to get the hostages back." Psychologically, the reason, whatever it is, has enabled the person to achieve a state of balance or homeostasis.

That seemed to be the main distinction among the people I spoke to in what justified a lie or not—if it helped or didn't hurt anyone, it could be justified, even if it might not be morally condoned or right. But if it hurt or harmed, it became a bad, unjustifiable lie.

In turn, such justifications can be used to shore up everyday business and social practices because they make the reasons given for lying in particular situations appropriate. Dick, the sales manager in a large company, gave an example.

I   I don't ascribe to lying. I don't condone it. But I think a good example of when it's okay would be a situation which occurred for a client of mine from the Northwest. He had a will agreement for all of the relatives to sign, and when he asked some of the relatives, he told them that another relative some asked about had already signed the agreement, and later that relative did.

Should he have said that? His view was that everybody was going to sign the document anyway; nobody got hurt by signing; everybody was going to gain from the document; and he was just trying to keep things moving and get it signed in time. And since everyone was going to sign—and did—why not do it as efficiently and effectively as possible? The results were exactly the same whether he directly told the truth, evaded the question, or massaged the truth as he did. So he felt his lie was justified. There was no cost to anybody; the lie didn't hurt anybody. So why not do it? At least that's how he justified what he did as being all right, and I suppose if I was in that situation I might, too, though I think lying in general is wrong, because it involves being evasive or not stating the truth as it is.

Then, too, a major justification for lying might be to serve some higher principle or good, such as the code of ethics of one group, country, or god. For instance, this is how Oliver North justified his own lies to Congress. He said he was serving a higher law to preserve the values of this country. It is an approach used by many others in the political arena to support their particular cause.

Sometimes religious leaders or other group leaders may use this, too. When Jim Bakker was promoting his fund-raising programs for his PTL organization, he would appear to have justified all his lies to himself in the name of his Christian mission or god. Thus it became all right that he sold more lifetime partnerships than could ever be accommodated; that he said he was raising funds for certain ministries and then turned those funds to other uses; that he bought this house or that with funds supposedly to be used for specific Christian works. And even hardened criminals use justifications to support their lies and crimes. Thus, whatever the nature of the lie, the individual explains it in terms of his own value system, so it becomes appropriate to use the lie. This helps to support the individual's own values by helping him to stay in balance—in homeostasis—with himself.

In some cases, this process of justification can even help the individual to feel proud of the lie, because he has been successful in using it to conceal something or to achieve a goal.

For example, Storm, the journalist, once used lying to get a woman he thought was particularly vicious in denigrating others to talk to him. As a result, she said things that discredited herself—a completely justifiable result from his point of view. As he explained:

I   I felt this woman was going around spewing out vicious stuff about gays, and even though I didn't think that she thought of herself as a vicious person, I felt the attitude of homophobia she was fostering was wrong. So I led her on to believe that if she talked to me for an interview, I would make sure that the world would get a chance to hear what she had to say and the interview would be unbiased. Which was true.

But what I didn't say is that I would ask tough questions, and I led her to think I would give her a supportive hearing. For instance, I told her she would feel better for doing the interview, and that the world would know where she really stood. However, after the interview came out, showing what she said she believed, she had tons of ridicule heaped on her; she lost three contracts and proceeded to divorce her husband.

I feel that was directly related to the article I did, and I was proud of it. She said all sorts of things in the article that turned people against her, and I was proud of what I did. Let's say I let out the red carpet and she walked upon it. She exposed herself for what she was, and I was very proud of what I did in setting the stage for her to do this.

Reactions to the Lies of Others

As much as we may justify and explain our own lies, we feel bothered or disturbed when others do it, except perhaps for the lies that have become everyday social conventions. When I asked people how they felt about lies aimed at them, the typical responses I got were: "I don't like it." "It bothers me when people lie, just as I don't like to lie to other people." "I don't think most lies are necessary—people could easily tell the truth."

Some people interpreted lying as a sign of lack of respect. Stan, the teacher, commented:

I   Well, I would always feel that someone really didn't respect me very much if they were lying to me, at least in the case of major kinds of lies.

   I don't feel this way about the run-of-the-mill sorts of excuses you sometimes get, such as when the kids in school fake a reason for an absence or someone doesn't feel comfortable saying their real opinion. But if someone close to me, such as a friend or colleague, was really lying about something serious, then that's what I think it would be—a lack of respect for me.

Others felt even more adamant about not wanting to hear lies. Susannah, a financial planner, felt "disgusted" by lies. She spoke with an intense fervor, the result of experiencing many serious lies in both her personal and business lives.

   I feel a great deal of contempt for the lie. My style is to want to get everything out in the open, and to confront things I feel aren't true. I know confrontation upsets a lot of people. They don't like to look at the truth. But I much prefer getting everything out in the open than dealing with someone who uses a devious, manipulative style, maybe because that was typical of some of the people in my family. So really, I hate it when people lie.

Nancy, the personal-growth counselor, summed up some of these feelings:

I   How do I feel about others lying to me? Generally, very badly. I immediately think they're on a very low level of development. And I don't want them in my life on a personal level. And in business situations, I have real high standards. If somebody doesn't come through that I'm doing business with, say I'm paying them money for something, I just don't give them any more business. If I don't feel a high level of trust for them or they don't keep their agreements, or if they're not into integrity, I don't want to deal with that.

It's different if clients come to me and lying is one of their problems, because they need to change that, and I help them with that. But I won't deal with it in my own business or personal life. I feel such people can pull me down, because their own level of development is low. So I would rather shut them out of my life.

Part II
Lying in Public &
Professional Life

CHAPTER 3

Everyday Social Lies

Some lies are so common that one may wonder whether they are even considered a lie, or whether they have become a social convention through which people offer comments, give opinions, make agreements, and give excuses that aren't exactly true—but no one really cares whether they are true or not. Instead, they are social glue.

On the other hand, there are people who do care, and they see such sloppy habits and imprecisions about the truth as a decline in manners and trust, as the tip of an iceberg showing a deeper lack of human integrity that threatens us all.

These social lies fall into six main categories:

○ the lies that cover up feelings and opinions;
○ the little things done to create a better image or appearance;
○ the agreement's made because it's easier to say yes when the real answer is no;

○   the excuses given to avoid activities;
○   the lies told to cover up forgetfulness and tardiness;
○   the little misrepresentations made to avoid or shorten undes-
     ired contacts.

Covering Up Real Feelings & Opinions

Perhaps one of the biggest uses for these common social lies is
to cover up how we really feel or think when we believe that our
opinions or beliefs may hurt or offend someone.

People ask: "How are you?" or "How do you feel?" They
don't really expect you to say how you really are. The usual
responses expected are "Fine" or "I'm feeling great." Quite
often, people don't even pay much attention to the response.

What if a person who gives the expected response really isn't
feeling fine? Is it a lie to say he is? Perhaps. But this is the classic
"white" or harmless lie, because the person who asks this question generally doesn't want to know the truth if the person isn't
feeling fine or great; he's not interested in the details, he's just
making a passing comment. Most of the people I spoke to and, I
suspect, most other people, go along with this convention. But
some people choose to break this convention and say how they
really feel when they don't feel fine. What happens then?

One of the people I interviewed, Roger the philosophy
teacher, had tried this from time to time as an experiment, and he
found this break opened new doors to communication. He did the
unexpected, and generally people seemed to respond favorably.

> Usually, when people ask you: "How are you?" they don't
> expect you to say how you really are. But I do generally. I
> feel I want to tell the truth if I'm asked, even if I'm not
> feeling particularly good at the time, so I do. So a lot of
> times I do tell people how I'm feeling. But if I'm not feeling
> particularly good, I'll try to say that in a comfortable way.
> For example, say I'm feeling depressed about something,
> and people say: "How are you?" Sometimes I'll make a
> joke about it and say, "Well, on a scale of ten, it's about a
> three." Or I might mention something that's recently been
> going on in my life, if this is someone I know.
>
> I have found that people do seem to appreciate the
> honesty. And it creates a new possibility for communication
> because I've broken out of the conventional. So much
> conversation is conventional. People think and respond in

routine ways. But then, when you break the mold, that
sometimes gets people thinking and reacting. I've found
it has helped to make some of the people I've used this
with more open and straightforward with me in return.

However, unexpected candor can make some people uncomfortable. Sandy, a marketing consultant, noted this had happened
to her at social gatherings. In response to her comment, "Oh, how
are you?" the person had started to tell her. "And I didn't like it.
And then I wasn't sure how to get the person to stop diplomatically, so I felt a little trapped into having to listen." But then
Sandy became trapped because she was lying with her question
and expecting a routine social lie in return.

Storm, the writer, often felt that friends who asked him for an
opinion were really looking for reassurance. As Storm commented:

Sure, I sometimes tell lies that don't hurt people or ones
that will make them feel better about themselves in
everyday social situations where the real truth is not
that important.

For example, sometimes a friend will come to me
and ask for my comments on some writing or other work
they have done, and I sense what they really want is
some kind of stamp of approval. They seem insecure
and they want to feel what they have done is okay.

Well, when they come to me like this, I won't say
this is terrible or awful, even though sometimes it is. Instead, I always try to put a prettier picture on it. In some
cases, it may be absolutely irredeemable, and in that
case I might try to tactfully make some suggestions,
though without putting their work down. For instance, I
might say, "I don't do it this way. This is how I do it."
And then usually, they take my advice.

On the other hand, when these social lies about feelings and
opinions might have some consequences in the relationship, people
might tell the truth.

For example, to save her feelings, Don, the engineer, would
often tell a casual girlfriend that he liked something she had
cooked when he actually didn't. But if this were someone he was
going to see for a while and she might cook what he didn't like
again, then he would say something so he would not have to
experience it again.

In conversations, people might avoid saying their real opinions or even state false opinions to help maintain the social peace. It was, as Blanche, the public-relations specialist, expressed it, a way of being safe.

I   I think people tend to be safe. They are careful, particularly when it comes to talking about sensitive subjects, such as religion and politics. A lot of people I know, for whatever reason, are careful people. And I find that they're very sensitive to other people's feelings and don't want to hurt their feelings. Also, they want to avoid saying things that could be controversial. A lot of people I know feel safer that way.

In fact, Blanche had a memorable experience at a prestigious dinner party. Her mother-in-law had reminded her not to talk about politics, because Blanche tended to be a fairly outspoken liberal, and this was to be a conservative gathering. Blanche found a way to break the taboo safely. As she described it:

I   It was a big society dinner sponsored by a conservative local newspaper publisher. My mother-in-law, who is very conservative, invited me, though I'm a liberal Democrat. So before the dinner, my mother-in-law said: "I don't want you to talk about politics." And when I asked her what I could talk about, she said horticulture. I told her, "It's fine for you to talk about horticulture, you raise cymbidiums. But I have very little to talk about if we talk about horticulture. But I will do my best."

Well, I remember wearing white gloves to this dinner, because it was that kind of event. And I also remember trying not to talk with my hands, because my father had told me that was always a dead giveaway as to my ethnicity and past. So I was trying to conceal that, too.

Anyway, I met the daughter-in-law of this publisher and her two friends at our table, and we got along famously. And then we were talking about cymbidiums, and I had very little to contribute to the conversation, and she looks at me, and she asks me why I'm not saying anything. And then she says there are only four of us, why don't we talk about something more serious? When I explained about what my mother-in-law had asked, she said: "Well, it's all right if I initiate it. Then, it will look like you are being responsive and polite." And so she started. And the two of us had a grand old time.

Creating a Better Image or Appearance

Creating a better image or appearance for the self can be fertile ground for social lying. Social scientist Ervin Coffman' points out how all of us have public and private personas, and he says that we create and play out our various roles on a kind of dramatic stage.

Some of the people I spoke to described trying out different roles or experiencing others doing this. In some cases, they found it enjoyable, like a kind of game, or a way of feeling more confident and successful by adopting such an image. But in other cases, they felt bothered by the deceptions involved in elaborating on what they saw as the underlying or real persona.

On the other hand, Sandy, the marketing consultant, emphasized the fun of role playing.

I   I sometimes like to imagine I'm someone else. So I'll go to a social event, and I won't tell people what I really do. I'll just be another personality for a while. I'll use another name. And I'll take on different traits to go with it. But then the other people I'm with will be aware that I'm engaging in this kind of pretense and they may adopt their own other self, too. It's like stepping into another role on Hallowe'en, though I might do this at an everyday party. And then afterwards, I step back into being myself again.

Others spoke of getting advice on image building from consultants so they would dress differently or change their speech patterns to attain a desired image. "And why not do that?" asked Barry, a management consultant I spoke with. "After all, if you create a certain image of success, people will tend to relate to you in the way you appear. And that will help you to become successful."

On the other hand, Roger, the philosophy teacher, and Raphael, the counselor and healer, had reservations about playing a part. Roger described his own discomfort in trying to misrepresent himself:

It happened when I was at a dinner party, and somebody asked me who I was, and I misrepresented myself. I was going to see if I could take this person in when he asked me if I was a member of some sort of debate group, so I said I was. I started out thinking it was a kind of game. But then, as we kept on talking and he asked me more questions about myself and the group, I just didn't feel very good about doing this. I felt bothered that maybe I might slip up, and I felt like it wasn't right to be trying to take him in. So it started to feel like a stupid game I was playing.

Raphael was bothered by the adoption of personas by others. As he commented:

There's so much posturing going on. There's men trying to assume a tough, machismo, I-can-do-anything role, and then there's people trying to look their best. There's so much secrecy. So many people not telling the truth of what's really going on. You say, "How are you?" "Fine. How are you?" "Fine." There's just so much superficiality in relationships. So much make-up and posturing.

It's like making up a résumé in a job search. You don't put on a résumé that you have a real weakness, such as getting unfocused, becoming really scattered at times, or getting very anxious. You want to look good and secure on your résumé. Just like you want to look good in social situations.

Avoiding Unpleasant or Undesirable Contacts

People may also use these little misrepresentations to avoid unpleasant or undesirable activities or contacts. For instance, people at a party use familiar getaway lines such as: "I just want to get another drink," or "Excuse me, I just saw someone I need to talk to." They cover up what could be the real reason for leaving—the person is a bore and they just don't want to talk to him. They might also use such lies to get out of going to some event in the first place, canceling out, or leaving early.

People also may use such getaway lines and excuses with strangers. Roger, the philosophy teacher, often did this to get away from panhandlers.

I   Say a panhandler comes up to ask me for money. The truth is that I'm unwilling to give them money. But I say: "I can't spare any," which means I can't afford to give, which is not true. But I'm afraid if I say I'm unwilling to

give them money, they'll take that as a hostile response,
and maybe they'll attack me, yell at me, or something.
So it's just easier to say I can't and get away.

And others reported coming up with their own excuses to
evade religious proselytizers, political promoters, and others
who approached them on the street.

Little Lies

These social lies are really quite common. Their purpose is to
make it easier for us to function and at times save face or help us
to make a better appearance. If there's something we don't want
to do, someone we don't want to see, a minor error we have
made, an appointment we have forgotten, a lie is often a handy
way to escape the consequences or give us an easy out. In turn,
people generally just accept these little excuses—even if they
know or suspect they aren't true. The situation just isn't that
important, and there isn't that much energy to confront everyone
on all these little lies.

But while these social fictions may not be that important,
they do raise questions about how they might contribute to a
larger pattern of lying about more serious things and to people
with whom one has a closer, more enduring relationship.

Lying in Public

*B*EYOND THESE EVERYDAY SOCIAL LIES, the next arena for lying is everyday public encounters—in stores, with salespeople and service people, with public officials and authorities, with neighbors, with landlords and tenants, with lawyers and politicians, and the like. In such situations, because people don't have intimate bonds, people may feel freer to lie. Moreover, many people already think the other person may be likely to lie to them. In that case, lying becomes like a game, a war, or a battle of wits.

Who Is Most Likely to Lie?

People have common suspicions about certain groups of people, mostly people in a position of power and influence who can use that power and influence deceptively and unethically. At the other extreme are disadvantaged people who are believed to use lying to get ahead or survive. I remember my parents telling me that we were part of the respectable and responsible "middle class" that was the backbone of the country, and they impressed me with the importance of following the rules. But then there were those people "up there" who took advantage and the people "down there" you couldn't trust—and I suspect these images of the upper, middle, and lower classes are still with us. In any case, those were the distinctions that emerged when I asked about who were more likely to lie—those on the top or those on the bottom?

The groups I heard mentioned again and again were salespeople, lawyers, PR people, and politicians—all people who use persuasion. It's no wonder such people tend to be associated with lying; they make their living by trying to outmaneuver and manipulate others, and maneuvering and manipulation are key reasons for crafting a lie. This doesn't mean these people necessarily lie. Indeed, lawyers have codes of professional responsibility, and others have codes of ethics.

Comments from the people I interviewed reflected these suspicions.

Roger, the philosophy teacher:

I   I usually expect salesmen to lie. Especially when I'm a customer for the first time. I feel that they may not tell me the full truth. They may not lie directly, but they may hold some things back. So generally, I try to be pretty wary when I'm first meeting a salesman.

From Alison, a counselor on personal growth:

For me, it's salespeople. People in real estate. You can't generalize. I work with some sales and real-estate people who are very spiritual and concerned about having integrity. But commonly, these people are into persuasion and manipulation, and that can lead to lies.

A man I encountered, a former lawyer now in real-estate sales, helped to confirm this impression at a cocktail party.

"I have a boss who told me and tells all his salesmen to say anything you have to to make the sale. That's the way to succeed in this business." Dick, the sales manager, who had introduced me, begged to disagree.

"I think in the long run, honesty and integrity pay."

Dick suggested there was a good reason for associating the salesperson with this image of deception. "I think the closer you get to a money motive, the closer you get to people lying."

As for PR people, Storm, the writer who frequently worked with them, had this to say:

| PR people, I think they lie all the time. It's an ingredient of the profession. They're always coloring or not saying things to manipulate the truth a little to present an image. I just think when you're dealing with a PR person, you have about a 90 percent chance they're going to be doing some kind of deceptive thing to some degree. Some are less hurtful than others; some want to lie less; some may not lie at all, though in my experience it's very few.

Lawyers? Joanna, a business consultant, and Jerry, a psychologist, expressed some of the common reservations.

> *Joanna:* I think lawyers are taught to be misleading. Even if they may not lie outwardly, lawyers still have to be an advocate, which means presenting their client in the best light. So they may not say something unless someone asks them directly. Or they will leave things out to give an incorrect impression. And often it's like they are playing a game, where the truth doesn't really matter, just who wins or makes the best point. And maybe that's their job; they're supposed to do this for their client. But it bothers me, and I think lawyers with their abilities to twist and shade the truth in creative ways are doing major damage to our country. They're undermining the basic principles of honesty and integrity, and I think in the long run we will pay for it.

| *Jerry.* The way I see it, attorneys have a relativistic ethic. They don't see lying as being an absolute wrong. Rather, the truth becomes relative. Maybe it's a gross generalization, but I would say generally, any attorney is paid to shape the truth by presenting one side of an argument. Maybe it's not a lie exactly, but it comes pretty close.

And then there were the politicians, perceived to be in a world where they were expected to lie to get ahead or to win support for their policies or programs. Stan, the high-school teacher, expressed a commonly held view:

| Politicians and lying! How can they not? That's part of the territory. I can't think of a president who didn't lie—for

sometimes good and sometimes not so good reasons. And I teach civics! Even with the cherry-tree story, Washington certainly told a few good ones in his lifetime. And we all know about the lies of Nixon, of Johnson, just about every president we've ever had. It all comes out.

Beyond the big four, there were many other groups that got a mention, including doctors and physicians ("They're reinforced, if not to lie, at least to conceal bad truths"), government officials ("Part of their job involves maintaining a good front"), and spies and CIA agents ("They're actually paid to lie and spread misinformation").

On the other hand, there were those "others"—the people perceived as a threat, the people out of the mainstream or in disadvantaged or minority groups—who were perceived as likely to be liars, too.

For example, one man thought there might be something in Oriental culture that encourages the lie: "Because saying no for them is very difficult; so you can say almost anything, and they'll say yes to it to agree, even though this isn't true. Or you'll agree on a price, and the job may take a little longer, so they'll ask you for more money even though you agreed on a fixed price." A woman I interviewed seemed to think lying was characteristic of Middle Eastern culture: "They're taught to bargain and cheat outsiders, so they can easily take advantage of someone who tries to be open and sincere."

Others suggested that people who were "poor and desperate for money," "on drugs or suffering from a chemical-abuse problem," "alcoholics," or people who were just plain "insecure" or "irresponsible" might be most likely to lie.

A feeling that a person must take justice into his own hands sometimes carries over into dealing with the phone company or insurance company. If people think the company has done them wrong, or if they think they might be hit with extra charges otherwise, lying might be a way out.

For instance, Dee, a real-estate investor, described how she used subterfuge to get the phone company to adjust a bill she didn't think she deserved.

0   I ended up with a large phone bill because someone had called me from Europe, and for some reason it got put on my bill, though it wasn't supposed to, because

this person had called me. But the phone company didn't want to take it off.

So I told the person that I was discussing the bill with that I was in law school, and I was planning to make this a test case for the phone company, if they didn't take it off the bill. And when I said that the company finally did take it off the bill.

So I lied, and I wish I didn't have to do it. But I felt I had to, because I felt I was right. The operator hadn't told me this was going to be a collect phone call, and then they put it on my bill. It was for $90, and I didn't feel like I should pay.

Raphael, the counselor and healer who sometimes works with social services, noted how he often encountered client deception. "They see me as aligned with the authority, so they don't tell me things, to protect themselves. Such as about child abuse, drug use, alcoholism, domestic violence, things like that, because if they tell me something, then it may get to the authorities, and they may risk having their children taken away from them. Or they might fear other penalties from the law."

Lying to Neighbors

Probably the one area where people didn't experience much lying was with neighbors, generally because people had little contact with them. If they had contact, it was usually the nodding-acquaintance variety. Blanche, the public-relations executive, expressed what seemed to be the most common feeling:

I   You know the old expression: Fences make good neighbors. So I don't know my neighbors very well, and I have fortunately never had a situation where any issue involving lying has ever come up. And besides, why would one lie to one's neighbor? There just doesn't seem any point.

But should there be a neighborhood problem or dispute, lying might occur. For example, I heard accusations of lying when I was a member of Community Board neighborhood conflict-resolution panels. This was a San Francisco community-service program in which a panel of three or four volunteers would help people mediate a problem. Typically, these were things such as disputes between neighbors over trees and noise.

One of the people I interviewed, Susannah, the financial planner, described a byzantine saga of deception, revenge, and legal wrangling involving a neighbor who claimed that one of her beautiful trees blocked his view. After she tried to work out an understanding by reasonably trimming the tree, he apparently decided to "trim" her tree himself while she was out of town. Let Susannah explain what happened:

II   My neighbor lied after he vandalized my tree, because when I went and confronted him, he denied it. And I know he did it, although I have no proof, because we have been battling about this tree for years. And I'm sure he lied, to escape possibly serious consequences for damaging my tree . . .

But in her own quiet way, Susannah took steps to deal with the lie, such as fantasizing that a large gorilla like King Kong stepped out from behind her tree, patted the top back into shape, and then went over to ravage the garden of her neighbors. And then one night Susannah quietly stopped by her neighbor's garden and carried out some of the things she saw the imagined gorilla doing, such as pulling up some of her neighbor's just-planted greenery. It was her way to quietly counter her neighbor's deception by being deceptive herself, although otherwise, Susannah would consider herself a generally righteous, upright, moral, and ethical person.

CHAPTER 5

Lying at Work

WORK LIES RUN THE GAMUT: employees lying to employers; employers lying to employees; co-workers and colleagues lying to each other. And there may even be institutional, company-wide lies in which certain procedures become a form of lying, such as the fiction of filling out forms and time sheets a certain way, when in fact, people in the organization are doing something else. Indeed, the work environment can often be especially conducive to lying because there is so much at stake. The need to keep jobs, earn more money, get a promotion, find excuses for problems with work, and jockey for position, prestige, power, and money can be an ideal germinator for lies.

For example, a company tends to lie in the name of efficiency to spur productivity, keep employees working, pass the buck, or evade being open about negative feelings, because it fears liability. Employees tend to lie to advance their careers, to protect themselves against mistakes, and to put down the competition. Co-workers often lie to shift blame or out of petty jealousy.

In turn, such a climate can encourage some people to form a series of temporary—or ongoing—and ever-changing alliances to gain support against the possible forays of others or to help in the attack or both.

But in certain work settings, such as when the company or employer tries to create a more open, supportive climate, such lying is apt to decline—because people have less to attack or defend.

Organizational Lies

Organizational lies usually occur when the usual rules or channels of an organization aren't working, so people go outside the system, which can create a lie when people cover up doing this. What makes it an organizational lie is that management knows about it and goes along, perhaps because it agrees with what people are doing or doesn't want to rock the boat.

Frances, a computer-systems supervisor, described how this often occurred in her own very large company in a few key areas—keeping time sheets, testing systems, reviewing employee performance, and dealing with promotions.

She began with the time sheets.

There's all kinds of fudging that goes on, and the company knows about it. This is the way it's done.

Basically what happens is we work 37-1/2 hours a week. But on the time sheet, we are supposed to show that we worked 40 hours a week. So what the company is doing is teaching its people to lie. Someone starts working for the company, and almost immediately they've got to fudge their time.

I don't really feel comfortable doing that, so I put down what I really work. Normally, it's 40 hours or more. But if I work less than 40 hours, which we may do, say because of a doctor's appointment, I put down what I did and any explanation.

But, then the others just go along with the usual procedures. Why not put down 37-1/2 hours and be accurate? We have quizzed our bosses. We have wondered why. We have guessed that maybe they're lying to upper management about how much everyone works, so it seems like people are doing more or getting paid less per hour. But they don't tell us anything—just to keep filling out the time sheets this way, which is a lie.

In some cases, this fluid approach to keeping time actually worked to Frances's advantage, such as when she was out for about a week, and her supervisor gave her some extra days' credit. Even so, she felt bad about it—as if she were collaborating in a secret company lie. As she told me:

> One time I had to have some tests at the hospital, and I thought I was just going to be there for two days, so I worked some extra hours before I did this to make up for this. But then it ended up that I had to take the whole week off, although I had expected to work it.
>
> Then, when I got back, I said to my boss that I probably only worked a total of twelve hours that week, including the time I worked on the previous weekend. However, he said, "Don't worry about it," and he put me down as sick for three days, so I could get paid for the whole week.
>
> The whole thing made me feel a little funny, because I find it hard to live with a lie. But then my boss thought it was okay, because that's the way things are done.

Employer Lies

When employers lie to employees, they may do it to protect the organization from a disgruntled employee, prospective employee, or former employee when the employer has to do something that person might not like—such as not hire or promote him, transfer him, or fire him. So sometimes it is easier to give another, more gentle, or diplomatic reason, than tell the blunt truth. Sometimes the lie involves liability. An employer might hesitate to reveal what's really going on because it might be used against him later in a suit. Another common lie is the lie to avoid embarrassment or save face when the employer has made a mistake and he doesn't want to lower himself in the eyes of his employee or employees. And sometimes employers may lie to suggest there is an opportunity ahead, knowing there is not, in order to get the employee to work harder or accomplish some task. In turn, since employers have the power, employees don't typically confront them over the lie.

But when employer lies get serious or pervasive, not only are employees more apt to provoke an angry confrontation and perhaps leave the organization, but such lies also are often what trigger employment-discrimination or unfair-practices suits. The employee who can't effectively confront the lie feels upset or angry about what happened and brings in the big guns to help fight the battle for him.

For example, this happened when Roger, the philosophy teacher, applied for a job. The department chairman gave him some administrative reason for not hiring him, when, in fact, Roger believed that the chairman liked someone else better, perhaps because Roger was something of a maverick.

As Roger commented:

I   I've been teaching in about a dozen different places for seven years, and I guess you could say I've sometimes ruffled some feathers, because I'm a pretty outspoken person. So it's true—sometimes people don't like me because I say what I think.

So that may be why I've had some experiences where my position has not been renewed after a year or where someone has decided not to hire me. But I don't always feel they really tell me why. I've asked, but often my experience has been that the person may not tell me what's so and I felt that he is withholding the truth, maybe because he'd rather say something safer to avoid hurting my feelings or provoking some kind of confrontation.

For example, a classic case of this type happened to me recently when I went to an interview at a university in a city near San Francisco. The man claimed he couldn't hire me after the interview because of some kind of administrative problem with the university—there were some limits on the number of part-time people he could hire.

Well, if that was so, why even interview me for a part-time position? I suspected that he just didn't like me as much as someone else. Finally, I cornered him and asked for the real truth—didn't he prefer these other people to me? Finally he told me the truth, that this was so. There were some limits on the number of people he could hire, so that part of his statement was true. However, he had also rated the people he interviewed. I rated lowest in the group. I imagine he tried to avoid telling me this to save my feelings or to avoid legal hassles later, but I preferred knowing the truth. And I think it's his right to not hire me because of not liking me. I just wanted to know.

Similarly, Dick, the sales manager, found it easier to give a phony reason for not paying an employee than to tell her he wasn't satisfied with her work. That way he could avoid confronting the situation. As he told me:

> A few years ago, I used to give my support staff part of my commission for doing a good job, and when this woman suddenly quit on me, she wanted her commission. Well, I was outraged that she would just quit without any notice, and then on top of this I thought it outrageous that she would expect a commission, too.
>
> However, I didn't tell her this. I just told her that I didn't have the money now, and so I wasn't going to pay her. Of course, I had the money, but it was easier to say that I didn't have the money rather than confront her and tell her how dissatisfied I was with her work.

Because Dick didn't tell her the real reason, the woman broke into his office to get the money. Looking back, Dick felt bad because he hadn't been honest with her in the first place.

> It was just a real embarrassing situation all around. A couple of weeks after I turned her down, she broke into the office, and no one knew why she was there. So when a couple of people saw her in my office, it got very emotional. She started screaming, saying that I ripped her off and stole from her and I owed her money. And then, when they called me, I just told them to let her go, so they just got her out of the office and we hushed the whole thing over.
>
> However, I felt very badly about the whole incident. I didn't feel good that she was leaving. I didn't feel good that I had been subsidizing her out of my own pocket to keep her there and then she left. And then I felt especially bad about the lying, telling her I didn't have the money, rather than telling her the real reason I wasn't going to pay her. I think if I had shared my real outrage with her in the first place that might have avoided her trying to come back to get the money afterwards. So her coming back made me feel even worse about the whole thing, and I wish I had just told the truth.

Setting the Tone

Besides lying directly to employees, employers can play a part in creating a tone or culture in the organization that can encourage or discourage lying.

For example, if employers create a competitive, closed, nonsupportive environment, it can contribute to lying by employees to each other and to the employers, because such a setting leads people to feel self-protective and defensive. So the lie becomes a shield to fend off threats and attacks and advance against others.

By contrast, if employers set the tone for a warm, open, supportive environment, it tends to discourage lying, because people don't feel the need to protect themselves and can share their flaws, mistakes, and fears openly and get support.

Judith Briles, who has written about corporate ethics, noted this important role of employers in setting the tone when I spoke to her. As she commented: "My experience is that when lies are going on, especially from the employer or person in charge, it contributes to regarding lies as an acceptable option, since the person we look up to, the person who we might want to be, does it."

Lying by Employees

Common employee lies revolve around exaggerating ability, experience, or power or making false claims about plans and intentions to get a job; using excuses or falsehoods to explain away delays and cover up mistakes, being late, or not working as hard as one should; and shifting the blame or getting revenge against someone else. Then, too, employees may lie because they have different values and priorities than their bosses, and the lie is a way to get what they want.

To Get a Job or Promotion

One of the most common and most socially acceptable employee lies is exaggerating past accomplishments to get the job or promotion in the first place. Then if you get it and carry out the task successfully, the lie becomes a *fait accompli—no* one discovers it or cares about it or all is forgiven after the fact. Sometimes the successful liar is even praised for his initiative and cleverness, except in certain fields where the discovery of the lie can destroy careers because of regulations and certifications required in those fields.

For example, Stephen, the writer, described a typical use of this approach, which he diplomatically calls "fudging."

) I may fudge a little bit when a prospective client asks me if I've had any experience in something that I haven't, say, insurance writing. I might say I have or talk about how I've written things in a related field that suggest I'm experienced in this area. So I try to get as close as I can.

To Make Excuses or Cover up Delays, Lack of Work, & Mistakes

Perhaps the biggest reason for lying is to excuse or cover up for something done wrong, at the wrong time, in the wrong way, or not at all. One person may do this to cover his or her own neck—or a whole team of people or even a whole division in a large company may get involved in the classic pass the buck, stonewall, or "I didn't do it, shift the responsibility" charade.

Briles, whose books include *Women to Women: From Sabotage to Support* and *The Confidence Factor,* describes this as quite common. "When people don't deliver what they say they were going to, they will often make up all sorts of stories covering up," she said. Yet, such lies, while common and unlike the lie told to achieve success, can be quite damaging to the employer or company. Not only may they damage quality of work, but they also can lead to more and more layers of lies, compounding the original problem. As Briles commented:

) As an employer, such cover-ups are not acceptable. If there's a delay, a mistake, a slip-up, I would want the employee to tell me what really happened. The problem is that excuses contribute to confusion and shoddy workmanship. For if you have this one excuse here, this other excuse there, another excuse over there, as an employer, you can keep entrusting getting the work done to whoever is supposed to do the work. But meanwhile, as the layer of excuses builds up, the slippage in production can continue and get worse.

And then, of course, there are those who lie to get out of going to work now and then entirely—lies of the "I'm sick" or "There's been a family emergency" variety when nothing is wrong. A local newsworthy problem may provide a convenient excuse for a way out, such as the San Francisco earthquake did for many people who weren't really harmed but claimed to be to get out of doing something.

Other lies are designed to pass the buck or escape responsibility. Such lies are rooted in people's insecurities and fear of losing face or being punished. When I spoke to therapist Sylvia Mills, she described lies of this type this way:

I   Many people lie because they are frightened of authority. They lie to cover up. A lot of people have problems dealing with authority and being up-front, because they may feel insecure or scared of losing their jobs. Or they may cover up because they don't want to lose face or they don't want to cause the loss of face for someone else. In other cases they want to pass the buck, which is very common. They deny responsibility, saying: "It wasn't me. It must have been someone in some other department." Blaming can sometimes facilitate their own work, because then someone else has to deal with the paperwork or problem. There's a lot of escapist lying in large companies or bureaucracies.

To Obtain a Forbidden Goal or Take Advantage

Employees also might lie to get something they shouldn't have. The classic example, of course, is the employee who embezzles and tries to cover up, which slides into criminal behavior. Often, employees lie and cover up to get other things too small to notice or make a big deal about, such as the employee who makes personal calls on work time, spirits away small quantities of office supplies, or uses the copy machine for his own work and then tries to hide his use. Or there may be somewhat more serious deceptions to gain something that the employer has expressly forbidden or which the employee knows is disloyal, hurtful to the employer, or otherwise wrong.

Alison, the counselor and workshop leader, described such a situation where a trusted employee violated an agreement that no staff member would date clients. But he did, causing her to lose some clients; and then when she found out about this and told him expressly not to, he did it again and tried to cover up, though she eventually found out and fired him. The lie and the act it covered up not only damaged her business, but Alison also saw them as a betrayal of a long-term friendship she had had with her assistant. As she explained:

II   I had an agreement with a male assistant that he would not date any female clients who showed up at my workshops. I made this agreement after I lost four or five clients who he dated. This happened because he would go out with them a couple of times, have a short romp with them, and then they'd be too embarrassed to come back after it ended, because they'd have to see him. So finally, after this happened four or five times, I made him make an agreement that if he wanted to be assistant for me, he couldn't date them. But he broke the agreement. And when I confronted him, he claimed he had totally forgotten that we had that agreement. But at the time we made the agreement, I made such a big deal about it that it's hard to believe he couldn't remember.

I didn't believe him and I fired him. I think if he had admitted or confessed what he had done, it might have been different. I might have forgiven him and given him another chance. But I felt not only did he break our agreement, but here he was trying to cover up and lie about it, too.

And this lie hurt so much, because this is somebody I had trusted so much in the past. He was someone who always had kept every agreement. He had always followed through and done everything he said he would do. I would literally trust my life with this guy.

As we spoke, I tried to stay calm, and immediately he offered to dump the woman, which made me feel even worse about the whole thing, because I thought: "Here he has lied to me about doing this, and this woman isn't even that important to him." Though later I found out he was still seeing her six months after he left me, so maybe he would have kept seeing her anyway and tried to lie about that.

In any case, that one lie was just so devastating for me that I had to fire him. And since then we've barely spoken. So it's very sad, and I feel this tremendous loss.

To Gain Alternate Goals or Priorities

Employees may lie when they have different ideas or priorities than their employers.

For example, Raphael, the counselor and healer, experienced this situation in his part-time employment at a social-welfare agency. The organization had policies about limiting treatment for clients after a certain number of visits. But Raphael thought a particular client needed additional treatment, and he felt it more important to fudge a little to provide that treatment than follow agency guidelines. And then he did some fast maneuvering to "cover his ass" when his boss had questions about what he did. As Raphael told me:

I   I've been having some problems with my current boss at the agency, because she hasn't let me get away with some things. She has been calling me on everything, including some things I have been doing to try to better help my clients. I've been going ahead with these extra services because I feel the clients need them, and I learned on an earlier job that if you think you can get away with something you believe in, do it, because it's easier to get forgiveness than to get permission sometimes in a bureaucracy. So I've done that, though it has created some tense times.

Lying by Co-workers and Colleagues

Just about any situation that evokes a cover-up or a desire for an extra advantage can trigger a lie between workers and colleagues. However, when co-workers work independently, have little interaction, or are in equal position without any reason to compete, there is little reason to lie.

In the interviews, some of the most common reasons for lies were: to conceal ignorance; to get others to front for someone who wanted to take some time off or who wasn't able to do some work; to compete for positions and promotions; to claim credit for something someone else has done; and to get even for petty jealousies.

Gaining a Competitive Advantage

The desire to get ahead or outdo another person can be another powerful motivator to lie. An employee can conceal his or her real interest in a position or promotion and secretly disparage other hopefuls behind their backs while professing complete support and loyalty on the surface. However, what is especially interesting about this competition is the way, according to Briles, that men and women do it differently. Both may lie or conceal the truth in the pursuit of a benefit. But more commonly, women will conceal their real interest from each other. By contrast, male rivals are more apt to declare themselves openly. As Briles told me:

/ Men tend to be much more overt about what they do; women more covert. For example, women tend to try to develop closer relationships and friendships at work, but they don't recognize that everyone is not friend material. So in wanting to develop this relationship and the rapport, one woman can give another the benefit of the doubt. But this can open up the women to being sucked in and taken for a ride by someone who is not really a friend, and it can leave her feeling more devastated and betrayed.

A good reason for this is that as women we grew up not only being taught to be nice and be pleasers, but we were taught to be friends with everybody. Also, we were taught that you don't compete with friends. So that leads women to tend to deny their attempts to compete with each other, such as when one woman announces she is interested in competing for something. Another woman who feels she is supposed to be her friend thinks she isn't supposed to compete. But then if she really wants something, she may compete actively anyway. But she just won't tell the woman who has announced her intentions about it.

By contrast, men tend to have the view that it's okay to compete with friends, and if you lose or you win, you can still be friends and go play racquetball or whatever after the game is over.

The result of this, as Briles explained, is that after the competition is over, the women who previously thought they were friends are likely not to be friends anymore, because the woman who announced herself openly will feel betrayed.

Undermining Other Employees

Still another source of lying between co-workers is the effort to undermine, put down, or "get" someone else out of jealousy, revenge, in battles for power, or for other reasons. Such behind-the-scenes battles are the everyday stuff of office back-stabbing or office "politics," as this is sometimes more gently and diplomatically known. And in some office settings, particularly where communication is closed and people play things close to the hand these battles to make others look bad so I'll look good can be rampant. But they tend to be less common where the office culture is more open and supportive.

In any event, such lies can be used as a web or trap to make the unwary victim look foolish, mistaken, or otherwise slip up. But those lies can also backfire, leaving the liar looking worse. Briles gave me an example of using lying to discredit another co-worker, based on her own research for her book on ethics in business. As she described it, one woman tried to make it appear as if another woman wasn't following through on her calls, so she would appear irresponsible. As Briles told me:

> **A secretary to the head of sales in a major high-tech company—let's call her Sharon—was pregnant and ready to go on a maternity leave. Shortly before she was to leave, her boss called her on the carpet for not following the company's policy that whenever an employee went on a break or to lunch, she was supposed to arrange to have her calls transferred to the receptionist, who would take them and then put any message on the company's voice mail.**
>
> **At the time her boss called her in, there had been a two-week period when Sharon hadn't gotten any calls, and Sharon had been surprised by this. Normally she expected to have a few messages waiting for her when she returned from a break or lunch. And now her boss was telling her that the company couldn't tolerate her laxness in having calls referred anymore, and if she didn't check out with the receptionist and stop leaving her desk and phone lines unattended, they would terminate her.**
>
> **Sharon was stunned, because she had been telling the receptionist to take messages and forward her calls when she left. After a little investigation, Sharon discovered what was going on. It turned out that another woman, who was after Sharon's job, would call the operator as soon as Sharon left and tell the operator to have all calls revert back to Sharon's desk, claiming that Sharon had asked her to pick up her calls. And then this**

woman would pick up these calls herself, and then she would go in to Sharon's boss and say: "Sharon is never at her desk, and I'm having to answer her phone all the time." So the woman was setting Sharon up and then telling her boss that Sharon wasn't doing her job.

How did Sharon deal with this?

Basically, Sharon dealt with it by confronting the woman. She told her that she had checked every day with the receptionist, which she had, and that she knew something funny was going on—essentially she told the woman she knew she was lying. And then she told her: "I'm not going to tolerate it any more." Then she handled it with her boss by suggesting there was some misunderstanding about the way her calls were to be handled. So she did handle this with some finesse and so as not to discredit the other woman, which might have made office relations even worse and backfired on her. But the woman knew Sharon knew what she was doing, and so, as Sharon told her, she stopped doing it.

As for her boss, he figured out what was going on and eased up on her.

And the other woman? What happened to her? Apparently, Briles indicated, the boss just let it go, glad that the problem had been papered over, although this incident might have tarnished the reputation of the woman who lied.

CHAPTER 6

Lying in Business

*B*USINESS IS ONE OF THE MOST COMMON ARENAS FOR LYING, perhaps because so much is based on the art of the deal, where doing well often encourages manipulation, posturing, managing impressions, and yes, deception to get ahead. In turn, much of this jostling to gain the advantage is considered part of the business game, permitted or encouraged by the rules, so often it becomes hard to draw the line between what behavior is perfectly acceptable and what behavior crosses the line.

Given this wide range for lying and this uncertainty about what is a lie, what are the major types of lies in business, and how do people feel about them?

There seemed to be major categories of reasons: lies because of money (to get out of paying, postpone paying, to pay less, to get more, to conceal a cash-flow problem), because of obligations (to get out of undesired ones or postpone them), because of information (to get it, to conceal it, or to cover up a lack of it), and because of mistakes (to cover up making them). Other key reasons for lying were to look better, gain prestige or power, or get business (say by showing off) with an ersatz self-image, exaggerating to appear in a better light, taking credit for something undeserved, and claiming an ability to do something and then not being able to do it (or not following through). There might be revenge lies for a business deal gone sour.

Lies to Look Good

People like to present themselves in the best light, and if a little lying will help—including taking credit where credit isn't due— some people will do this, particularly in business situations where the stakes are high.

This kind of lying might be considered, as Owen Edwards calls it, "less as lies than as the truth improved."' It is probably in this one area that people in business have the most trouble in deciding whether something is a lie or whether it is a positive shift of emphasis to show oneself off to the best advantage. As Edwards observes:

I   Perhaps this penchant for counterfeit self-improvement is a universal trait. Psychologists have begun to suspect that some illusions about our worth may be essential to maintaining mental health.[2]

Indeed, as Edwards comments, this self-puffery is learned early in life, because "we learn that being seen in a favorable light has its rewards. People are impressed, attention is paid, and we are well liked."[3]

The business consultants and therapists I spoke to agreed that, within limits, this "spin" is fine from various perspectives—as an accepted practice in the business world; as a moral way of elevating the self as long as one's intentions and underlying purpose were good; and as a psychologically healthful thing to do.

From the psychological point of view, therapist Sylvia Mills seemed to think that such positive presentation of self was quite healthy as long as a sincere intention was there and the claims were in keeping with reality. As she commented:

I   What's the line between out-and-out lying and talking "as if," which is one way to program yourself for success? According to this principle, for example, you talk as if you are confident or successful. Sometimes I use these positive affirmations.

I think the key distinction between this "as if" talk and a lie is the person's intention. If he is presenting himself in a certain way to cover up something or mislead somebody in some way, then that would be called a lie. But if a person is doing it for himself, such as to improve himself, by saying "I'm very successful," or "My book is doing fantastically well," I don't think they're lying. Rather, they're living in expectation—which is fine.

In fact, some psychologists make tapes for people to help them build self-esteem, and these tapes encourage them to present themselves in a very positive way. For instance, they may be asked to repeat and keep thinking to themselves: "I am confident." They're not confident in the beginning, but when they play the tape over and over and keep asserting that thought, they'll believe and therefore become more confident. So I think this kind of self-presentation or affirmation can be used for reprogramming, which is a positive.

There is a point, Mills agreed, when such self-presentation becomes a lie. That point was elusive, but it seemed to hinge on the intentions behind the image—combined with a dose of reality. If the person wanted to make a certain impression that was misleading and he wasn't working on his own internal programming to make that impression a reality, then this presentation would be a kind of lying, because, as Mills put it, this person would be "living in fantasy." Then, too, if the person always knew his goal was impossible, that would be a lie. As Mills put it:

I   If a person truly believes he can achieve it, even if he can't, then that's not a lie. But if he pretends to be someone he has no intention of becoming, then there's deceit on purpose, and that's a lie.

Between these two extremes, it's a matter of degree when something becomes a lie. It's a matter of quality and quantity.

For example, I regard myself as an honest person. Yet sometimes I get involved in this kind of behavior—it's certainly not daily or even weekly. Its quantity is small, so is the quality. There's not an enormous discrepancy between the person I really believe I am and the person I'm trying to be.

It's a little like if I'm late; I'm likely to be just five or ten minutes late, not three hours. Similarly, when it comes to the presentation of self. I'm basically the person I say I am, and if I exaggerate, it's by very little. But if somebody tells big whoppers to brag, then that's another situation. The farther you actually get from reality, the more likely something will be judged to be a lie or deceit.

Because this potential for "legitimate" and "illegitimate" posing exists, it is always a good idea to check things out before buying any kind of service or dealing with anyone who claims to be a professional. Look for inconsistencies between actions and claims, and listen to intuition or gut "feeling."

Taking the Credit & Making Can-Do-It Claims When One Can't

Other common lies involve a person taking the credit due to someone else or claiming he can do it when he can't or when he doesn't follow through.

In some cases, these "take credit" lies are accepted—such as when a boss gets the credit but the underlings do the work. I think we would have to call them institutionalized lies—socially accepted and endorsed perhaps. But still they're lies.

On the other hand, there are some areas where "take credit" lies do become viewed as harmful. When they involved writing or art or people's ideas, these lies can turn into plagiarism, which is punishable by law. Such lies might occur in an office where, in the course of jostling for position and promotion, one person takes the credit or the glory for another's work, while someone who should get credit does not.

Lies for Revenge

Lies committed for revenge when a business deal goes sour or other personality conflicts surface are definitely beyond the pale. These are clearly malicious, evil-minded, hurtful lies, ethically acceptable to no one. A person may use such lies against another, intending to hurt, yet at the same time concealing the lies, because he knows there could be serious legal consequences. There may be one exception: After the lie succeeds, the person seeking revenge may want the victim to know that he is responsible.

The Case for Honesty & Ethics in Business

While lies may lead to success in the short run, honesty and ethical dealings can contribute to long-term success based on trust and fair dealing, as well as contributing to the social fabric as a whole. Many of the people I spoke to, for example, commented on the way honesty in business was simply the pragmatic thing to do.

For instance, Dee, the real-estate investor, told me she would never lie in a business deal. Why?

> I   Because I don't see the advantage in lying. It will only backfire eventually when the truth comes out. And if you enter into a business relationship with someone, that's likely to happen. Maybe not immediately. But sometime. And then that cannot only damage the business, but people who lie in one deal create a trail that can follow them to hurt them in business deals in the future. They may even end up injured or in jail. So there's really no pay-off in the long run. It's better to be straight with people in dealings up front.

By the same token, being honest can be a way of getting the help one needs in business. Robert Middleton, the small-business consultant, found this in his own practice. Business people often would try to posture to make it seem as if their business was going better than it was. But to get help they would have to be open about what was going wrong. As Middleton commented:

> When someone comes to me as a client, at that point I find that people are ready to tell the truth because it's not working. Their survival is at stake. They realize that they have to trust someone, and so then they open up quite a lot and will answer just about any question about what they're doing, how much money they are making, and the like.

Another business consultant, Dave, found that being open and honest about his own needs attracted people who could support him. He had tried to play the expert who didn't need people, because he felt that helped to increase his own stature. But that tended only to isolate him and make him more vulnerable, and he actually gained strength by admitting his own vulnerability and need for help. As Dave told me:

I had a real breakthrough when I decided to open up and let people contribute to me and support me. I had pushed people away before, because I had this conception of myself as the expert, and so I felt that people couldn't contribute to me, because I was supposed to be the one contributing to others because I was the consultant.

But once I started telling the truth about that to myself and opening myself up to others, a lot of contributions started to come in. Before I had been saying "I don't really need anything from anybody," which was absolutely untrue.

Some of the things they contributed to me were ideas. For example, they gave me ideas on ways of conducting my business and how I can charge for my services. Then, too, I had been trying to deny that I needed any help financially, and once I was willing to recognize this, I got some help from my father. I wrote to him, telling him that I needed some financing and gave him a plan of what I was going to do to extend my business, such as advertising and putting on workshops for larger companies. And I told him that "I would love to be supported by you," and he gave me the money I needed.

So as a result, I've been able to take my business in a new direction. Instead of doing so much one-on-one consulting and working on particular small projects with businesses, I've been doing more workshops, which have also been very successful. I've been able to contact and work with the larger companies. So, without all this financial help and these new ideas, this may not have been possible.

And then there is that need for ethics, because it helps to make one feel better about oneself. It's a source of self-respect, a point that Michael Josephson, the president of Joseph and Edna Josephson Institute for the Advancement of Ethics, made in a recent speech on making ethical decisions in business. As he stressed in his talk: "Ethics is not entirely personal. Ideals of ethics are universal, they are timeless, they have existed forever." He said one of the first qualities essential to ethics is honesty, which means being trustworthy, and that is different from being truthful, because truly honest people don't deceive, while professionals might mislead people without ever lying.

It's a nice sentiment to be left with as we contemplate the potential for lying and cheating in business today. But is a more ethical, honest approach possible? Josephson observed in his talk: "In an immoral world, doing the right thing is not rewarded." But do we live in an immoral world? Is the business world based solely on a Wild West, survival-of-the-fittest, to-hell-with-morality ethic? Or is there really an underlying code as well as a pragmatic value in being honest, trustworthy, and sincere? I'd like to think there is.

Part III

Lying in Personal & Private Life

CHAPTER 7

Lying to Friends & Relatives

HEN WE LOOK AT LYING to friends and relatives, we move from the arena of public life to the more personal and private sphere of life. To a great extent, the rules about lying change; it becomes more taboo. The closer the relationship, the greater the sense of betrayal when a lie occurs, although many lies may be excused or forgiven because they were designed to protect or help another person.

This initial chapter in this section focuses on lying among friends and relatives. Future chapters deal with closer types of relationships—between single men and women; between spouses or partners in committed, live-in relationships; and between parents and children. These chapters illustrate this pattern or correlation between closeness and lying and point out the loss of the relationship and trust that a lie can bring about.

Lying to Friends

The people I spoke to had little experience with friends lying to them or lying to friends themselves, because friends, by their very nature, are people with whom one voluntarily chooses to have a relationship. Indeed, some people select others as friends because they feel they can be open and honest with them and trust them.

The lies committed were usually of the helpful, supportive, white-lie variety, such as telling a friend he had made a good choice or had good taste about something, when one couldn't agree less.

Storm, the writer, made this point when he told me:

> Sometimes my friends have engaged in some lies to help me. For example, when I had a drinking problem, some of my friends who knew helped me out by covering up for me from time to time. Or they may have lied to protect me from knowing something that would hurt me.
>
> But if someone engaged in any lies to hurt me, he wouldn't be my friend for very long. For instance, if I thought a friend was trying to steal from me or was doing something out of revenge, I wouldn't continue to consider him my friend.
>
> And, yes, that sort of thing has happened to me a couple of times. Someone I trusted who blew that trust. But then once someone does something like that, then that can break the friendship forever. It's hard to restore that trust which is the basis for friendship, and you just write that person off your list.

As Storm made it clear, he didn't want to have as friends people he couldn't trust.

Similarly, Blanche, the publicist, characterized friendships in much the same way. As she put it:

> There are all kinds of friends in the world, from the social friends to the deep, close friends. Well, with social friends, you might expect some of the usual trivial lies, like excuses when someone can't make some event, and those are no big deal. But then, with deep, close friends, I think a lie would be terribly hurtful. You don't expect it from them. You expect them to be honest, trustworthy, and sincere.

Some people even thought that the basis of a good friendship was the ability to tell a good friend everything, the bad along with the good. For example, Sarah, the educator, voted for complete honesty. As she commented:

I I just don't want to have someone in my environment personally or professionally who can't be straight and up-front and live their life honestly. I just feel if people are friends, they should have integrity in their total relationship, in every moment.

I know many people feel that the white lie between friends is okay, such as concealing some information so someone's feelings don't get hurt. Well, I have a hard time with that. I think that puts up barriers in the friendship. It's like keeping secrets from a friend, when I think the essence of true friendship is to share.

For example, say you learn that a friend's husband is fooling around with someone. Some people I know would say: "Why should you tell them? Why is that your responsibility? Why should you hurt their feelings?" Or say you learn something about their job that might make them feel bad. They would say to keep this from them to save their feelings as well.

But I think that's baloney. I think you should feel free to tell friends what you really know or think. I think good friends do this for each other, and that's what makes a true, real friend.

While lies among friends may be less common, friends do lie, and there tend to be certain types of lies that are most likely to occur. First and most common, there are the benign and supportive lies of help and protection. Second, there are the little lies that are more like humorous or entertaining exaggerations, and which add vitality to the friendship.

But then there are those that threaten it, such as lies that occur when a person is undependable, or the lies that occur when a person violates some basic rule of the friendship (such as breaking an agreement in order to do something else that sounds better and making an excuse to avoid revealing this to the friend). Perhaps the most damaging lies that involve friends are those that arise over money.

Also, there are those lies involved in breaking up the relationship.

And finally, for people who have a higher level of expectation for the kind of openness and revelation a close friend should share, there may be lies when the other person is more concealing than expected. For instance, Raphael the healer, who was more sensitive to such things, had this to say.

1   I think it's pretty common for people to hold their real
feelings back and not say things sometimes, which I see
as a kind of a lie. For example, friends may not call me
when they are hurting, or people may not call me when
they are angry with me, or they may not write to me and
let me know what's really going on, such as any judgments that they have about me, if they have judgments. I
think that happens because people want to stay more
removed. They don't want to get into a discussion about
such things. They don't care enough to go through with it.
Yet I think that's an important part of a real friendship.

   I have a male friend who's a dancer I respect. He's
been very honest and friendly to me, and usually he's a
very warm person. But also I have sometimes gotten
this feeling of distance. And sometimes I have wanted
to say to him: "Jack, I would really like to know what's
going on. Are you feeling withdrawn from people generally? Is there some reason you feel like pulling away
from me?" But it's scary for me to do that. It's like
maybe making an issue of something where maybe
there wasn't an issue. Or maybe just bringing this up
might make him uncomfortable, so, instead of relaxing
the relationship, it might put more stress into the relationship. I did this once and it helped to clear the air,
but it's still a scary thing to do, because there is the
potential for making things worse instead of better.

Lies to Help & Protect

To make a friend feel better you might say, "You look good,"
when the friend really does not. Or you might lie because the
knowledge would be worse than the lie or because you feel you
have no right to interfere, such as when the friend is unaware
that his person's lover or mate is cheating on him.

   While some people may feel that friends should be completely,
even brutally honest, many others would temper that honesty with a
dose of caring.

   Storm, the writer, described how he appreciates the deceptions
of his friends.

I   Normally, I don't lie to my friends and my friends don't
lie to me. We wouldn't be friends if that were true. And
there are certainly types of lies that people I call friends

wouldn't tell to me or I to them. For example, in the writing game, some writers might stab you in the back, because they want to get a story or cover their own ass about something. But I don't operate that way with my friends, and none of my friends do with me either.

In fact, there was one time when some of my friends lied to me to help me with my alcoholism, and later on, I was glad they did this. Basically what they did was conspire secretly behind my back to get me to go to this treatment center, including talking to my dad and getting him to agree to come out and take me down there. I didn't know they were doing this at the time, and later I decided I needed to go there myself. But when I heard about what they had tried to do, I really appreciated it. I felt they were really showing love and trust and faith in what they were trying to do.

Lies to Embellish & Entertain

Other lies that are okay among friends are those that are done within limits to exaggerate and embellish in the name of amusement and entertainment. Such lies are harmless and benevolent. Perhaps the other person is aware that this is a lie—really a tall story or an exaggeration—and goes along with it because he enjoys it.

Blanche, the public-relations executive, said that she frequently used this kind of lying with her friends, and that whether they knew the truth or not, they enjoyed going along with her stories. As Blanche commented:

I do embellish. I tend to hyperbole, to exaggeration. I once had a client who called me a dissembler when I said something to make him look less silly by turning a situation around to make him look better. Now a dissembler is a term fora liar, but the way he said this, I could tell he was saying this in a friendly, kind of kidding or teasing way, because he knew I was doing this to try and help him.

Also, some of my friends have called me "dramatic" because I tend to build things up. I take things that from their eyes are very undramatic and make them bigger, because I don't see the world in this flat way. For example, I might tend to say something like: "It was really wonderful!" or "She's so awful," when I don't really mean it was all that wonderful or that she was that awful. It's

just an overstatement to dramatize, to make things
seem more exciting.

Why do I do this? Because I tend to want to be
amusing. It's almost the same thing that a comic does. For
example, I'll embellish by turning a story around to have a
funnier ending. Or I'll exaggerate to make things more
interesting. For example, say somebody doesn't look that
good, I might say something like: "Oh, you should have
seen what she wore. She really looked like the Medusa
with her new perm and all her gold jewelry."

These lies were okay because Blanche kept them within acceptable limits. Beyond that, a friend might be seen as a "pathological liar" who exaggerates and distorts everything and whom no
one can trust.

Lack of Dependability & Follow-up Lies

While these helpful, benevolent, and fun lies may generally be okay,
there are other lies that threaten the trust so central to the
friendship.

One common type are the lies or promises friends tell about
things they are going to do, but then they don't follow up. The lack
of certainty, dashed agreements, and wasted time and efforts that
result can seriously damage the friendship.

Some friends may seek to compensate when a friend is
undependable but there are other things they value in the friendship. Yet even here, the lack of dependability may place barriers on
the depth of the friendship. This happened to Alison, the counselor
and workshop leader. As she told me:

I   I have this friend— I'll call her Francine—who has
trouble keeping her commitments or being on time for
things. For example, once in a while she'll say: "I'll call
you real soon, and we'll make a date for lunch." But
then it will turn out that it won't be real soon because
she gets hung up with other things sometimes.

My other problem with her is that she is always late,
so I can't depend on her. But I have found a way to
compensate for this by either setting the time we get
together earlier so she'll meet me when I really want. Or
I'll use humor when we talk about this to try to give her
the message to correct this.

But then, because of this problem, I don't do as much with her as I would do otherwise. For instance, different things will come up and I know that we'd have a good time together. But I'll ask a different friend or I'll go alone because I don't want to hassle with the time problem.

Money Lies

Among the most damaging lies to any friendship are lies about money—to get it, to avoid giving it up, to pay less, and the like. When a friendship is linked to these money issues, the conflicts that arise over money can destroy the friendship.

In some cases, of course, money can help a friendship—such as when one friend loans money to support another—as long as nothing goes wrong (the money is returned) or there are no unfulfilled expectations (such as when a friend loans money, hoping, but not expecting, that it will be repaid). But most money lies and the conflicts that result are destructive.

Alison, the counselor and workshop leader, for example, had a "friend" who continually forgot her wallet, so that Alison had to pay for everything, and her friend never paid her back. Though Alison continued to go along with this for some time, because she enjoyed these evenings with the friend who had little money, the ploy made her feel resentful. As Alison commented:

It bothers me that people sometimes take advantage and manipulate you through lies. There was one time when I was about thirty and a single parent, and I was in a needy space that a friend took advantage of. This woman and I would go out together about once a week, and that was my salvation. This was a chance to go out and have fun, let loose, and maybe meet some guys. Well, the way she took advantage of me is that every single time we'd go out, she'd always forget her wallet. Every time. And I would have to pay for her. After about sixteen times, I realized I was being taken.

I would overlook it. Why? Because if I didn't pay, it would crimp my good time, and I didn't want to do this, because I had a baby sitter, and this was like my big night out. So it was worth it to me at the time just to come up with the extra money to cover her. Then, too, I guess I went along with this, because I knew she didn't have a lot of money, and this is how she survived.

Roger, the philosophy teacher, described how a friend, who worked as a fireman and became wealthy as a real-estate investor, lost friends over debts.

II   Once he gained his money, Bob had a lot of friends come to him for help, and they promised to repay it. But then they didn't, and he lost friends that way.

Maybe they felt that because he had money they didn't have to pay him back. But he didn't think that was right. He told me that since he has a lot of resources, he's willing to share a certain amount of them, and so was willing to loan small amounts of money to people on an interest-free basis. But he has insisted on being paid back on time.

Otherwise, he feels that people are trying to take advantage of him, and get out of an agreement they made. So he's lost friends as a result. But then, I think that's right, too. People shouldn't think that just because a friend has more money that they have a right to that money because they're a friend. That's when a friendship can run into trouble. The person who borrows the money starts to think he shouldn't really have to pay it back because his friend has more. But the person who loaned the money did so because he both wanted to help his friend and the friend agreed to pay it back. So no wonder he might be angry when the friend doesn't do this. He feels the friend broke the agreement intentionally, and he feels ripped off.

Lies to End the Friendship

Finally, there are lies used when people feel angry with a friend or uncomfortable about ending the relationship, want it to be over or less intense, and don't want to reveal these feelings to their friend. So there are excuses, postponed meetings, unreturned or delayed calls—anything to avoid a confrontation and help the relationship slip away without a messy end. Frances described this process with one long-term friend she wanted to break away from. As she told me:

II I have a friend that I have a real difficult time being with, because I feel we live in a lie. Nothing has ever been straightforward with us, and I just want to be out.

We've known each other for about fifteen years. And during this time, she has always had a lot of money problems and I find myself very frustrated about this because she'll approach me to get help. But then I also don't want to run her life or tell her how to run her life. But she always seems so needy that I have felt like I should give her some guidance; so I find the situation draining and I feel pulled in two directions.

That's why I have come to feel the situation is impossible, and I just would rather be out of it. I'd rather not even see her, not even talk to her. And yet I'm very uncomfortable about having these feelings, too.

So that's where I've created these little lies to avoid saying what I really feel—that I don't want to be around her. So when she calls and says: "Do you want to do something?" I've been busy. Or one time when we did get together for lunch, I seemed distant and distracted.

So gradually we have just drifted apart, and I think she has gotten the gist, and hasn't called me for a long time. So it's been easier that way. It just seems like we've grown out of the relationship, without there being a sudden break and it has felt easier that way.

Lying to Relatives

When relatives turn into friends, because they have things in common and do things together, the usual patterns for lying to friends apply. Otherwise, relationships with relatives are quite different because of blood or marriage connections. But at the same time these relationships can range from the very distant to the very close, the possibilities for lying go through all sorts of permutations.

Lies of Avoidance

In many cases, people just aren't close to some of their relatives, so there is relatively little reason to lie, unless something pops up, such as an inheritance dispute.

However, once there are less acceptable reasons to avoid or reduce contact with the relatives, the lies may begin. For example,

Sandy's real reason for not wanting to see some of her nearby relatives was that she did not like them. She didn't like the way they had tried to impose their own values on her when she was a child, by expressing disapproving noises to her mother, so when she grew up she wanted them out of her life. But her mother, who was still in touch with these relatives, didn't want to let the relatives know the real reasons, so she found excuses to cover up, such as "Sandy is too busy" with this or that. A few times she persuaded a reluctant Sandy to send greeting cards. But even after Sandy stopped doing this "as a favor to me," as her mother put it, her mother still tried to maintain a face that said all was well.

Similarly, Raphael, the healer, encountered denial when he spoke to his cousin soon after his father and his cousin's father had a business fight.

	Jack, my cousin, assured me that he didn't have any animosity toward my parents after what happened, although then he said something like: "Well, what your mom said didn't help matters." And then he said again that he didn't have any animosity and wished them the best of luck. But I didn't really believe him, and I said that: "I really don't believe that, I'm not sure I believe you."
	However, he didn't really comment on or acknowledge what I said. I felt good that I said that, because it was truthful. But I feel he was just trying to hide his true feelings.

Finally, the lies themselves sometimes provoke avoidance.

For example, Sandy reported that her parents effectively isolated one of her aunts who repeatedly exaggerated and lied about little things.

	My mother used to tell me all the time about how my aunt lied about everything. She would say that things cost much more than they did. She would talk about her wealthy relatives and her connections with royalty in Europe, when none of that was true. She would claim that she had ins in the publishing and film business, when in fact, she just had a relative in a lower-level position who had very little power. She was constantly bragging about this and that, and my parents didn't like it. So they avoided her as much as they could, though of course they didn't tell her why directly. They just

found reasons why they would be busy so they could decline dinner invitations and they stopped inviting her to most things, too, other than general family gatherings, where it was hard not to invite her and her family.

Similarly, Storm, the writer, reported disconnecting from his own relatives who lied, though in his case, there seemed to be a whole parade of people who lied. As he described it:

I   I have a family of cousins, uncles, and aunts that is just full of liars. So I don't have anything to do with any of them. There are very few people in my family I'm close to as a result.

     Some of my relatives are just crazy. I have one aunt, for example, who just doesn't know what she's saying. She's so insecure. She builds all kinds of fantasies. And then the other relatives—it's unbelievable the lies, deceptions, cheating, backstabbing, trying to steal property—it's like a whole "Dallas" scene though on a much smaller scale back in the Midwest, because they don't have that much money. But that kind of stuff has been pervasive in our family—it's a kind of small-town—type politics atmosphere.

     So from the time I was a child, I never got close or connected with any of my relatives, because it was so obvious they were a bunch of hypocrites, and I'd hear stories from my parents or other people in town, or I'd see what they were doing. Or then other people would report what they said about something, which wasn't true. So the lies would get back to us.

Lies to Impress

Relatives may lie, too, to impress other relatives. Such lies are often born of a struggle between relatives to show how well they or their children are doing compared to the others.

Sandy, the marketing consultant, had parents who did this constantly, particularly her mother, who was a real social striver. As Sandy told me:

I   My mother always wanted to seem very successful, more successful than her three brothers, so she was always exaggerating what I or my father did, or concealing things she thought were not so good, so we would fit the image she wanted to present.

For example, when I was first starting my business and my mother sent me some money to help finance things, she continued to tell everyone about how well I was doing, even though I was still not making it financially, and she never let on she was helping to support me. Then, later on, when I managed to send her back a few hundred dollars on a loan for about $50,000 she had given me over the years, my mother announced that I had sent her this money as a birthday present and said nothing about the loan.

Lies about Money, Jealousy, & Revenge

Finally, there are the more intense lies that arise among relatives over money or when bitterness develops over things such as jealousy or a desire for revenge.

Dick, the sales executive, described how one of his customers manipulated his relatives to get them to sign an agreement about a property that had been in the family for more than a hundred years.

0   It's amazing. This client has bragged to me about how honest he is in business with his customers, and he says that's why he has been able to build up his business so he had become the largest distributor in the state. He doesn't lie, he says, so people trust him.

But then, as we were driving to the airport, he described how he had just sold his ranch, which had been in the family for about 120 years. And he had to get his relatives to agree to sell it in order to get the money and distribute the shares. Well, the way he went about it, he said, is he told each of the relatives that all of the other relatives had signed, though they hadn't.

"But isn't that dishonest?" I asked him. "Here you've been telling me how you built your business on honesty," and he replied: 'Well, the way I look at it, there are shades of honesty, and I don't lie to my customers. But in this case, I don't think my relatives are very bright. They're idiots and I can't wait to get rid of them. So I felt I needed to shade the truth a little to get them to sign. And I don't see this as a real lie because everyone will sign eventually. The lie will become the reality, so it's okay to say something if it's going to happen." And he didn't really understand that this was a lie.

For sheer drama, perhaps nothing compares to the story told by Susannah, the financial analyst, of family betrayal, revenge, jealousy, money, and suicide—a painful illustration of the tragedy that can occur when a family's lies explode with emotional intensity. But let Susannah tell it:

‖   My sister lived in a fantasy world half the time and was mentally ill. She would tell the most outrageous lies, though she would tell them in the most sincere fashion. I think that she honestly believed they were true.

    The biggest one that led to the rift between us was when she tried to back out of a contract she had signed by claiming that she had not signed it; that I had forged her signature. It was a contract that when my mother died my brother, sister, and I would distribute the estate equally, which was drawn up by my father, because he felt that my mother would not leave me anything, since we had always been alienated. So instead of compensating for this in his own will, by leaving me more, my brother and I persuaded him to do this, because we thought this would contribute to more harmony in the family.

    But when it came time to honor this contract, after my mother died some years after my father's death, my sister reneged, claiming I had not signed the contract, which would have meant paying me about $20,000. Well, eventually I sued, and when the handwriting experts we both hired agreed that it was a legitimate signature, I won the case and I ultimately collected, including damages. But after paying all of my legal fees, I came out about even.

By the time of the contract incident, Susannah and her sister had not spoken for about seven years, so all the communication about the contract agreement occurred through her sister's husband, who answered Susannah's letters since her sister wouldn't answer them herself. Meanwhile her husband contributed to the tapestry of lies as well. As Susannah described it:

11   After my mother died, I wrote to my sister to see if she would honor the contract, and when she didn't answer, I

spoke to her husband several times. He claimed she was very shaky, very upset over the death of her mother, "So we mustn't press her" —the same kind of solicitous nonsense I had been hearing all my life.

So I backed off for a while, though after about a year or so, my lawyer told me that if I was going to sue, I better go ahead and do so. So I tried writing one more time and this time my sister made a suicide attempt— something she had been doing for years as a way to get her way. Usually, she would slash her wrist or take pills, though this time she shot herself. Well, my brother-in-law claimed she had done it because of the pressure I had put on her over the contract, and then he called me about once a week for the next two months to tell me that if I didn't back off, my sister intended to kill me.

Well, I believed him and backed off completely for the next three months, because after all, I thought, my sister could do this, since she had a loaded gun. However, when the case finally came to trial, I discovered that my brother-in-law had really lied about this to get me to back off. What had happened, as came out in testimony, is that my sister had only made the threat to kill me one time right after she had made the suicide attempt and was in the hospital. "I'll kill her," she said. But then, when her husband called me, he kept repeating this threat as if she was making it week after week. So he was trying to intimidate me so I would back off.

Finally, several months later, she really did commit suicide, although it would seem that the real reason is because her husband decided to leave her and had moved in with another woman. Though she dated a number of other men after that, his leaving left her really depressed. But then, in her suicide note to the police, she blamed me and the lawsuit, which was really a form of lying. Her very last act, and it was a lie. My lawsuit had occurred about six months before, while her husband moved out about ten weeks earlier. And when I met one of the men whom she had dated afterward, he told me she had been quite disturbed by the break. So I'm sure it was that. But she couldn't acknowledge that, and we had been warring for so long,

since childhood, that it was easier to blame her suicide
on me. She had been blaming things on me all her life,
so why not her final act?

Thus, lies with relatives can sometimes become extremely intense when they are fueled by long histories of blame, competition for family love, and jealousy, as illustrated by Susannah's story. But more commonly, they tend to revolve around money, impressing one another, or finding ways to gracefully get out of having contact when the relatives don't like each other, but don't want to admit it.

CHAPTER 8

When Men & Women Lie

The Dating Game

ANOTHER COMMON AREA FOR LYING is the dating and mating game. Perhaps that's one of the reasons it provokes so much lying—because it's a kind of game. People negotiate and bargain over whether there will be a relationship and what kind it will be.

People lie to themselves about what they want and whether the person they are seeing really fits this image. They lie to get to see someone—or to get out of a meeting. There are lies about making and breaking dates. Once people are dating, there can be lies to avoid intimacy. People who are dating or trying to date may lie to exaggerate their prestige, power, or personality.

And then there are the lies—more commonly committed by the male—to get sex or more sex or better sex.

Men use strategies such as the normalcy argument (i.e., Sure, everyone is doing it); hiding his marital status; concealing some type of deviant sexual interest or illness; or pretending to use birth-control devices. Women may counter with their own form of sexual lying—telling the man how great he is when he isn't.

Both may lie about not seeing others to preserve an illusion of true loyalty. Finally, there are the most bitter lies of all, which can destroy a relationship, or often occur as the relationship is falling apart. These are the lies about money; the lies during fights; and the lies about endings—often committed because people hate confronting each other or the truth when things are breaking up.

Lies to Yourself

Several of the counselors and therapists I spoke to pointed out that lying in the dating relationship frequently begins with lies to oneself. What commonly happens is a kind of exaggeration in which the suitor creates an ideal person and then measures the people he or she meets against that ideal. The result is usually frustration, because the real person fails to measure up. A common fantasy for men is the young, beautiful, sexy woman. But for some men such a woman is unattainable, because they lack the trading cards in the dating relationship that are generally needed to attract such a woman. The men may be old, unattractive, or not have very much money themselves. So they dream. Conversely, some women dream of that attractive, successful man with money. But with many of these attractive, rich, successful men being drawn to the young, beautiful, sexy women, many ordinarily attractive and successful women are just not going to land these men, either. Thus, they feel frustrated, too.

People may have more specific fantasies and illusions. Susan Scott, a relationship counselor, pointed out:

Many people have fantasies. They'll meet somebody, and they'll make it into something that it's not and build an illusion and fantasy around it, rather than really look at it, tell the truth about it, and recognize that this really isn't what they want.

For example, say a person who wants to remain where he is meets a person in another state. He or she really wants to have a relationship with someone who lives within a hundred-mile radius. But then he or she spins a romantic fantasy about the new relationship that is doomed to failure. After all, how are they really going to create a relationship they want under the circumstances? It's an impossible relationship to begin with because he's not going to move and she's not going to move. But they each may create an illusion that the other will. So they kid themselves about where the relationship is going, when it isn't going to go anywhere.

Others may build up the relationship into more than it is because of their insecurities and fears of taking a chance on getting what they really want. This is what happened to Raphael, who described how his lying kept him in an unsatisfying relationship for more than two years.

|| Sometimes I have fooled myself to get into or stay in a relationship that I know isn't long term, but I would like to believe it is or will be. So I have concealed the real nature of the relationship from myself. For example, I stayed in a relationship once for two-and-a-half years that I knew wasn't right and I knew I had to get out of it. But I couldn't muster the strength to say: "Look, this is something we need to talk about. We need to end the relationship." I was afraid of hurting and rejecting the other person, and also feeling alone myself by making the break. So I just kept it going. But the real heart and love had gone out of the relationship for me. And I think she knew it. But I think she was fooling herself, too, because she was also afraid to make the break.

Lies to Avoid Getting Involved or More Involved in the Relationship

Men and women seem to differ over the roles they play in initiating the dating process or moving it on to a more committed relationship because women tend to make up excuses for not getting involved in the first place (usually to avoid hurting the male's feelings), while men tend to find reasons or excuses to avoid getting more involved (usually because it's the woman who's pressing for commitment or intimacy).

Getting Out of Dates

Generally, it's the women who make excuses to get out of a date, because they don't want to hurt the man's feelings by saying no outright or giving the real reason for the rejection. But whoever the person saying no is, the goal is to be diplomatic and gentle.

Reba, a speaker and seminar leader, well expressed this spare-the-feelings approach when she commented:

> Well, if someone called me to go on a date but I wasn't really interested, I might say something like: "I'm really flattered," but then I would probably make up something, such as "but I have a boyfriend," or "I'm busy this weekend," rather than say: "No, I'm not interested." I would do this rather than be direct, because I'm afraid I'd hurt their feelings otherwise.

It was easy to do this because the man would normally accept the rebuff and not try to press for the real reason.

Susannah, the financial planner, gave a good example of a typical lie she might tell, in this case an excuse about the things she had to do to avoid getting involved with a married man.

> I lied to him just this morning. He's a nice man who's been a friend for about a year, and he comes over from time to time to help out around the house for me. He does things like repairing the electrical switches and wiring. I'm really grateful to him for doing that. But he's a married man, and I have no interest in a romantic relationship with a married man, so I've always kept things at arm's length. And in the past he hasn't pushed things.
>
> However, recently he has been having a really hard time, because he just lost his job and I think his marriage has been under stress. It's just a sense I have, because he doesn't talk about this.
>
> Anyway, he called up this morning and wanted to know if we could get together this weekend. And I have been at some group social gatherings with him in the past. But this weekend he wanted to get together just with me by going out to a movie or dinner. But I felt that was too much like a dating situation, which I want to avoid with a married man. So I just made an excuse about the things I had to do. I felt like I wanted to let him down easy, because he's emotionally vulnerable right now, and I feel like I'm in a sticky situation. I want to give him some support while he's unemployed, as a friend. But I don't want to get trapped into something that's going to be emotionally sticky. I thought the excuse was a good way to keep things on the even keel they've been on.

While the women I spoke to may have seen this kind of gentle turndown as a way of saving the man's feelings, some of the men felt bothered by what they saw as women being devious or wanting to avoid a confrontation about the truth. For example, Roger, the philosophy teacher, felt this kind of upset over such lies most strongly.

I   It sometimes feels like the woman is giving me the runaround, and it bothers me. I just think it would save everyone a lot of trouble if she'd tell me how she feels up front.

For instance, I experienced a very painful example of this recently. I saw this woman in the hallway at the college where I teach, and I was very impressed with her. She was very attractive and I felt she had this strong sexual, passionate energy; she was just incredibly striking, and I wanted to get to know her.

So I followed her to her office and found out where it was. And then a few days later, I walked into her office and said: "You don't know me, but I'd like to introduce myself." It was a real bold move on my part, something I don't normally do, but she seemed receptive to getting to know me, although now looking back, maybe she was just flattered that I would go to such an extreme length to get to know her.

Anyway, after I introduced myself, she mentioned briefly that she was single, never married, and had one boyfriend, but nothing exclusive. So we made plans to get together. But then, she called to cancel, saying that something had come up that she had to do. And then I said, "Fine, well, let's set another time," and she asked me to call her to do so.

But then, when I did, I felt like she was trying to evade me. One time she said: "Oh, my boss is calling me so I can't talk now." Another time, she was just busy with work. And the third time she gave me her home number to call her there, but when I did, she said: "I can't talk to you right now, I've got company over." And the next time, it was: "Oh, I'm waiting for my cousin to call; I can't talk to you right now."

So after a while, with all these reasons, I began to think she was just putting me off. So I wrote her a card, hoping to find out what was really going on, and I said: "I get the impression that you're not interested in going out with me. And if that's true, fine, but I'd just like to know. Please let me know whether you really are interested or not."

And she did call back. But she seemed very defensive when I told her I was feeling very frustrated that it had been so difficult to talk to her. I had the feeling that she really didn't want to see me after all, from what she said. However, she was also very upset that I had seen through her and tried to confront her about this. So I thought that she just basically wanted to call to smooth things over and make peace, though she also didn't want to see me.

Another time, Roger was upset by a woman who took off without explanation after they had agreed to a date after getting connected through an ad. He described his frustration.

I   I had joined this date-by-mail service, and every so often I'd get a response from a potential date in the mail. I got this one from a woman who looked pretty good, and I called her and we talked on the phone for two or three times at the office where she worked. She was a professional in the biology field, and we had both had Ph.D.s so there seemed to be a good match.

Anyway, we arranged a date, and she agreed to come over with the wine, while I was going to get the bread. And then we were going to go out. It sounded like a kind of romantic evening—maybe too much for somebody one doesn't know.

Anyway, when I got there, a little late, I'll never forget the expression on her face. It's like when she saw me, her face just fell. She had this look of total disappointment, and perhaps this was because I hadn't had a haircut in a while, because the man who cuts my hair had been hit by a car, so my hair was a little shaggier than usual. Anyway, whatever it was, I got the impression that she didn't like the way I looked, though she didn't say anything.

Well, we went inside, and we had this real tense conversation, though we had had great rapport on the phone, and then we talked about where we would go to have the bread and wine. We finally agreed on a nearby lake that has a public park, after she turned down the first place I suggested as being too isolated. And then, when I asked, "Whose car shall we go in?" she suggested that we take separate cars.

I thought this was a little unusual but agreed, and then she agreed to pull her car around, and while she waited in front of the house, I went to get mine. But when I got back after a few minutes, she was gone.

I felt really devastated by this. What had I done to offend her? I wondered. And when I called her and asked if I did anything to offend her, she just said no. So she wouldn't tell me what bothered her. Was it because I was a few minutes late getting my car and meeting her? Was it because she didn't like my appearance? Whatever it was, it really bothered me that she wouldn't say. Maybe this was a case where she was withholding the truth to save my feelings. But I felt it made it worse. Not only did her driving away bother me, but her not telling me why bothered me even more.

Similarly, men finding themselves in an undesired dating situation might attempt various tactics of diplomacy to avoid being direct—as several women reported. Some common ploys:

◯ One man in an introductory phone call with a woman suddenly claimed to hear the doorbell ring and said he would call her back, but never did. "God knows what I might have said to dissuade him," said Sandra, the marketing consultant who told me about this. "I was just answering some question of his when suddenly I had the sense that he turned off, and I think his excuse of the doorbell was his diplomatic way of saying good-bye."

◯ Another man, on a first date after responding to an ad in a local single's paper, suddenly remembered he had to check to see whether he had left the lights on in his car. When he returned, he said he had to take the car to a garage. The woman who had just met him didn't, of course, believe him, but what could she do?

◯ In another case, Sandra and several of her women friends had a dinner party for some of the men who replied to a single's ad. They thought they had screened the group carefully, based on the letters and in some cases photos the men had sent. But it turned out that one man, who had sent a picture that didn't really look like him and had used a false name, knew two of the women already and seemed not especially interested in talking to the others. So during dinner he made a point of talking about how he not only worked in the cellular-phone business, but carried one with him, and he said he sometimes got calls for emergencies where he had to call his office. Then, a few minutes after dinner, lo and behold, he claimed he heard his phone beeping, though no one else did, and he quickly ran to a phone in the kitchen. Then, according to one of the women who was helping to clean up the dishes, he went through the motions of pretending to make a call to his office. After a few minutes of this, he emerged triumphant, saying how sorry he was, but he had to leave early to take care of some unexpected important business at his office. And then he left, saying how much he enjoyed the evening, though everyone else clearly knew the truth, and for several minutes talked about his elaborate attempted ruse. Why couldn't he have just told the truth?

As these stories illustrate, in early dating situations, people will sometimes go to great lengths to avoid admitting the truth—that they don't like the other person and don't want to get involved. So why not just call to cancel? Or let the other person know gently that they aren't interested? Generally, the passive resistance is viewed as easier and more comfortable. The person really wants out but doesn't have the courage to say what he or she really feels, commonly because he or she wants to spare the other persons' feelings or just doesn't want to risk an unpleasant confrontation.

Lies to Avoid Intimacy

In the later stages of a relationship, other lies may be used to avoid intimacy. Here it is generally the men who come up with such lies, since it is usually the women who want a more committed intimate relationship.

Susannah reported this sort of problem. She had been dating Allan on and off for several years, and at one time broke up with him because she felt he wasn't as serious as she would like. Now they were back together again, but though he talked vaguely about how he would like to get married—sometime—she felt the same lack of commitment from him, an unwillingness to talk about it, and the use of various ploys and lies. It was Allan's way of avoiding a messy confrontation about the nature and future of their relationship while keeping it going at a more casual level. As Susannah commented:

I   Allan often used these little white lies to get away from
      me or avoid facing the truth about things. For instance,
      he would spend Saturday night here, and then he'd get
      up on Sunday morning and would suddenly say, "Well,

I've got to leave. I've got to go to work." Then, I might ask him: "Allan, what kind of work are you going to do on Sunday?" and he'd say, "Well, I've got a whole bunch of things I need to take care of."

Well, I found out one time when he did this, he really went home and turned on the football game and spent the whole day in front of the TV with beer watching football.

I think the reason he did this was he was avoiding intimacy, which is what I sometimes accused him of. Paradoxically, he couldn't stand being around me on a protracted basis, even though he kept talking about wanting a relationship. So at the least bit of pressure, he would slip away. I feel he did this because he doesn't know himself. He's very confused and mixed up.

Lies to Exaggerate, Show off, & Increase Self-Esteem

Many people in dating relationships lie to exaggerate, show off, or impress others with how terrific they are. It is a way both to build their own self-esteem and to get the other person to respond and give them what they want. As the common equation goes, men use these strategies to get sex; women use them to get a more serious, committed relationship.

Sandra, the marketing consultant, described how one man she knew regaled his new women acquaintances with tales of all the property, jets, and yachts he owned—when he owned none.

Others may lie to seem more exciting and daring.

For instance, a man Dee dated described how he went through a fire and was burned all over, along with other stories of great adventures. Dee was quickly able to see through the guise.

I could tell he was lying about the fire because I was a nurse then, though he didn't know it. So I asked him to show me his scars, but he didn't have any. And I knew he would have to have them if he was burned as he said. So I knew he was lying. And I guess he was doing this to impress, but didn't know I had the background to see right through him.

While such exaggerations of self may be blatant, other exaggerations may be more subtle, puffing, or slanting to appear in a favorable light, so that the line between what is true and false can become very fine indeed.

Raphael, the healer, described wrestling with this issue in his effort to lead what he considered a life of integrity.

I   I'd like to be more honest, but sometimes I wonder if it's completely possible. For example, with this current woman I've gotten involved with, the day I met her, I had led a dance workshop involving dancing and moving. I told her about doing this and I said I like to consider myself a dancer.

But then, thinking about it, I wondered: Can I really consider myself a dancer? Is that really accurate? Is it a fabrication? Is that more of a fantasy? Am I really a dancer, or a therapist doing workshops on dance or movement?

These things can sometimes be hard to define, and generally, I try not to fabricate with friends. If anything, I try to be really open about who I am, and I feel I admit more of my weaknesses than most. So I think I'm more honest at that level than most people.

When I spoke with clinical sexologist Louanne Cole, she noted that men tend to exaggerate about money and family connections. And men often exaggerate their sexual conquests, a point that Dick, the sales executive, made:

I   You know, men sometimes make things up about women, such as that they've been to bed with someone. It's a way of showing off. I experienced this just last night when a gentleman I introduced to this lady told me some things I knew aren't true. They've only known each other for a month and have only gone out twice, but he told me that they've already been in bed together. But knowing the woman, I find that incredulous. I know her well enough to know that's not her style. She needs a more long-term, committed relationship first.

By contrast, women tend to use exaggeration and manipulative tricks to show off their popularity and desirability to others, as relationships-counselor Susan Scott described. For example, a woman who has a man visiting her might have someone call her on the phone every hour or so, so it appeared as if she were popular. Or a woman might pretend to be busy when a man called. In fact, I remember learning such tricks from my mother and girlfriends as part of the dating game. It was part of playing hard to get to exaggerate my self-worth and thus make the male think me more worth getting. Indeed, a woman I once worked with pretended to have another love interest and threatened to break up with her long-standing boyfriend because he didn't want to get married. In this case, her exaggeration worked and he married her because he decided he didn't want to lose her.

Persuading by Use of Lies about What Others Do

Doctor Cole calls these lies of persuasion "normalizing lies." The idea is to persuade someone to change his or her behavior to what others do or to embarrass him or her from doing something by claiming it is not normal to do or be or think that.

Cole gave me examples, many used by men to get sex or a particular kind of sex from a woman who was hesitant. For instance, the man might argue that "others are doing it" to persuade an unwilling woman. Or if the woman said she didn't want oral sex, he might say: "If you don't enjoy oral sex, there's something wrong with you. You're not normal." Conversely, a man or woman—though more commonly the woman—might use such a normalcy lie to discourage some sexual behavior, such as claiming: "People who look at pornography aren't normal," or "Using some kind of sexual accessory isn't normal."

While such statements may definitely be false, they may or may not actually be lies, because in some cases the person using this technique may actually believe the statement. Rather, he or she is just calling some common behavior normal as leverage to win the other person over, a little like a lawyer using a particular spin or emphasis on evidence to win a case. Whether a real lie or just leverage, this technique can be effective, because, as Cole pointed out, "most people want to be normal. So when someone else convinces them that a certain way to act, think, or believe is normal, they want to conform."

Still, some people may challenge the "normalcy" claim. When they do, there's a risk of jeopardizing the relationship. But they are willing to do so for the sake of standing up for themselves. Otherwise, according to Cole, if they are afraid of losing the relationship, they will go along with their partner's normalcy claim, whether they truly believe it or not.

And then what? What is the challenged person making the

claim likely to do? Sometimes the person making the claim is only bluffing, pushing the partner as far as they can to get what they want until they hit resistance. When this resistance occurs, they are willing to back off, because they want to maintain the relationship. On the other hand, the person may want this goal so much that if his or her bluff is called, the relationship will end. As Cole commented:

> The response is extremely varied. In some cases, the relationship will end; in other cases, it will not. For example, say the man argues for oral sex, using the normalcy claim, and argues that "If you don't give me oral sex, I'll leave this relationship, because I just can't imagine being in this relationship without it." Then she doesn't give it to him. Sometimes he may stick around, but find another alternative, such as getting oral sex on the side from another woman or a prostitute. Other times he may forgo his sexual desires. And then still other times he may leave.
>
> So there can be a lot of claims of leverage that are not followed through on, though there has been an ultimatum. But at other times, the claim is true. And then the relationship will end.

Lies to Conceal an Important Truth about Oneself

Still another common lie in dating is the concealment of an important truth about oneself to initiate, maintain, or deepen the relationship or to get sex. One of the most common ones is claiming one isn't married when one is or one is getting a divorce when one isn't—usually done by the man. Or one may state that one hasn't had a sexual relationship when one has—usually a lie told by women. Another reason for lying is to conceal some deviant or undesirable trait or behavior—such as one's age (usually done by women) or one's liking for some unusual sexual activity (most commonly told by a man). Still other examples might be concealing or denying problems or weaknesses such as alcoholism, using drugs, a lack of earnings, sexual difficulties, and the like. Then, too, other common concealments or denials might revolve around past relationships—how many, how often, even how lonely or how desperate one is—in order to be with someone.

Dee described several instances in which her girlfriends were courted by a man who turned out to be married. These men usually were concealing their affair from their wives as well.

A lot of my friends have been taken in by married men who have been cheating on their wives. And then they say they aren't married. So they're lying to their wives and the women, too.

For example, one girl told me the married man she was going with was going to leave his wife. But in the beginning, she didn't even know he was married; she thought he was already divorced. So when she did find out, he told her this "I'm-going-to-leave" story. However, though she wanted to believe him, it seemed pretty clear he would never leave his wife, and I told her that. Why? Because he had secretly seen other women on the side. And he already had three children. So why should he leave? Even if he didn't really love his wife anymore, he would probably have to give up 50 percent of his income to her in child support and maybe in alimony. So any divorce was unlikely.

And finally, after several months of his stalling, she realized this was true. He was just lying to her because he was interested in her for sex, so he pretended to her he was the available guy she wanted. But the reality was that he was really married and intended to stay that way. And finally she found this out. And she broke up the relationship when she realized this was true.

In Reba's case, she concealed prior affairs from a man whom she was afraid would be jealous and maybe break up the relationship. As she described it:

I   In my last relationship, I didn't want to tell him I had a couple of affairs. So when he asked me if I had done this, I just said no. I thought he might be angry and it might hurt the relationship or he might leave.

Eventually, he did find out, though I didn't tell him. He heard it from some person I used to be friends with who got mad at me because I had mistakenly revealed something about him, and when he found out, this was like his way to pay me back. As it turned out, the man I had been seeing was quite upset about this knowledge about me, so I feel I was right not to tell him early in the relationship when he asked me, though I don't like to lie. However, by the time he found out, the relationship was really ending anyway, and this helped to end it.

Though eventually we made our peace about this and now we're just friends.

So should I have been honest in the first place? It bothered me to lie at the time, and I talked to a couple of my women friends about this. But they said: "No, what's done is done." So I never told him myself. But I still think what I did is a lie.

As for the lies used to conceal deviant or undesirable traits or activities, Susannah, the financial analyst, described how one man had concealed his interest in being a transvestite (a liking to dress up in women's clothes) from her. She thought this a significant concealment because she doesn't consider this normal. In fact, it was one of the factors that contributed to her eventually breaking off the relationship. As she explained:

I   Jerry didn't exactly lie; but he didn't tell me he was a transvestite. At one point, perhaps, he hinted at this, when I asked him if he had any idiosyncrasies that I should know about before he moved in with me. Well, at the time he mentioned that his dead wife Joyce had a skirt that he liked to wear around the house. When I asked him why, he told me it was because it was more comfortable, since pants can be very hot, and air circulates under a skirt. So, because he and his wife were about the same size, he sometimes wore her skirt.

Then, because the skirt belonged to his wife, I asked him: "Please don't bring any of her clothes with you when you move in." So he didn't. But the first time I did his wash, I found all these women's underpants. And when I asked him about it, saying: "I thought you promised you wouldn't bring any of Joyce's clothes with you," he told me: "Oh, those aren't Joyce's. I bought them through a catalog."

So that's when I realized that he was a transvestite. But he hadn't told me that. And I didn't like his not revealing this. I felt cheated. On the one hand, in an intellectual sense, I felt he had a right to do this, a right to have his own lifestyle. But at the same time, I don't get sexually turned on by transvestites. I don't like men who dress up. So this materially affected my relationship with him after I discovered this. And I probably would not have invited him to move in with me had I known in the first place. So I'm sure that's why he didn't tell me. He thought if he told me I might change my mind. But then when I found out, I eventually decided to break up the relationship anyway.

While Susannah may have been sufficiently turned off by this behavior that it contributed to her ending the relationship, in other cases, the initial concealment might provide time for a relationship to develop, so that later this deviation might be accepted.

For example, Harvey, a doctor I met when I was doing research on a community of people experimenting with erotic dominance and submission as a lifestyle, did this quite successfully.' As Harvey described it, he enjoyed being submissive to a woman and engaging in various forms of S&M and bondage-and-discipline play. But when he first met a woman, he didn't tell her this, because he felt she would think he was weird or sick. However, as he got to know the woman, he would drop hints, and then if she seemed responsive, or at least receptive, he would let out a little more. If not, he would back off.

For instance, he might mention that he had seen a movie recently or heard someone relate a fantasy about something, and what did she think about it? Gradually, if the woman seemed open, he would lead up to sharing and acknowledging his own fantasies and eventually he would get her, if willing, to participate with him in acting these out. In turn, he found this strategy worked because the woman got to know him and came to see him as an otherwise ordinary, normal, respectable person, so that as he gradually revealed his real interests, she was willing to accept them, because she had come to accept him.

Similarly, Don, the engineer, concealed his herpes condition when he first met a woman, to permit the relationship to flower, although eventually if the relationship turned intimate he would reveal this. He explained his approach and justification:

0   I've met some women through personal ads I've placed in a local paper, and I've been mostly honest in describing myself. But I did decide to leave one item out—the fact I have herpes. Because I felt if I put this in, women might not answer this.

However, I felt it was okay to do this. Why? Because my rationale was that if this information turned out to be important, because a committed relationship develops, then I will reveal it. But if it doesn't turn out to be important, because the relationship isn't going anywhere, then I won't. There's no need to reveal such personal information in that case.

Other Lies to Get Sex or
Avoid Uncomfortable Discussions about It

Still other lies are used to get sex or to avoid talking about it in a way that might be uncomfortable.

A good example of this is the way men—and usually it's the men who tell these kinds of lies—lie about their interest in the woman to get sex. They pretend they are more interested than they really are and want more of a relationship than they really do. Women, on the other hand, are more apt to use sex to seek a relationship or more intimacy.

In a sense, the man may be honest initially because, excited by the power of sex, he really does anticipate the beginnings of an enduring relationship. But then, after the sexual experience, he may feel satisfied, so the desire for the relationship recedes. So what was the truth may turn into what seems like a lie, when it's actually the paradox of differing male and female cultural training or biology.

In any case, these kinds of male reassurances made about the future to get sex now are common in the early stages of many male-female relationships, since men tend to have a more recreational attitude toward sex—"Let's have fun now"—while women tend to have a more long-term view of it—"Will we see each other again?" or "Do you love me?"

In turn, these kinds of male lies or promises can add to the uncertainty that women tend to feel in the early stages of a relationship, as sexologist Louanne Cole pointed out.

For example, a woman hears him say: "That was wonderful," or "I'll call tomorrow." At this early stage of the relationship, she may be unsure whether it will continue and whether she will hear from him again. So she may wonder if she became sexual too quickly. Should she have waited? And if she doesn't hear from him, she may worry about whether things might have been different if she had put him off.

Meanwhile, the man promises to call, but he doesn't. In some cases, he may have the intention of calling, but other things come up. Or he may just say he will call to help protect the woman's feelings. Or his promise to call may be a strategy just to gain sex, since he thinks the woman needs that promise to be willing.

And what if he told the truth? In Cole's view, it might be nice theoretically if he could express his desire for short-term recreational sex, so the woman could agree on this basis. But many men don't do this because they don't want to take the chance that the woman will say no. As Cole put it:

| Say the man lies about his future interest in a woman to get sex now. He's taking the risk he might sully his reputation if she tells others what he did. So he's weighing out the benefit of sex now versus the risk of the bad reputation and being thought ill of by the woman when he doesn't call.

It's a weighing that happens very quickly. For example, if he decides to lie, he may think to himself: "Oh, she'll never tell anybody; she'll be too embarrassed." Or maybe he'll think: "I don't care what she says; I don't know any of her friends anyway." Or perhaps he might decide: "So what if the woman hates my guts. Who cares?" And then, seeing no risks to telling the lie, he goes ahead.

The women hearing the lie may respond in various ways. Some may acknowledge that the man is seeking just recreational sex, even if he hasn't stated this directly, and agree that this is fine, even as she is going along with his game that they will see each other again.

Other women may think that although he really is seeking just recreational sex now, even though claiming otherwise, once he has sex with her, he will want to form a relationship with her. In Cole's view, this thinking is often a delusion, because the woman doesn't know the man's inner desires and intentions. Also, such an attitude is often a kind of "magical thinking," based on believing that the man will change his interest to something more permanent or committed just for having the sexual experience with her, when in fact, many men tend to have the opposite reaction, feeling that if something comes too easy for them it's not worth much.

Thus, caught between the uncertainty about lies and truth in the beginning of a dating relationship, women walk this delicate line in trying to figure out what's too soon or too impetuous and what's just the right amount of waiting and assessing, if their purpose in the encounter is to build a relationship. For some men, this uncertainty contributes to the conquest mystique or excitement of the chase that stimulates their libido.

Complicating this whole equation are the women who would rather hear the man go through the pretense of "I'll call you," when he has no intention of doing it, because, according to Cole, they don't want to face that reality so soon after having sex with a man, because they would experience that as demeaning. Others would rather hear the truth right away and not sit waiting and wondering whether he's going to call.

Another common male lie might be the claim to be "safe," so the woman can't get pregnant, although the men I spoke with about this didn't think such a lie was either common or justified, because of the potential dangers that a pregnancy might bring. Still, one of the men, Roger, the philosophy teacher, had used this, hoping there would be no bad consequences, and not feeling good about telling such a lie later. As he described it:

I   I don't normally lie to get what I want in a relationship. That's not my style. I try to be very open and frank. But I do remember one lie I told and I didn't feel good about it. What happened was I was seeing this woman and we usually had intercourse with condoms. But one time, I got carried away and didn't have anything on. Well, she thought I'd used a condom, though I had not. But I didn't tell her that I had not used it, because I knew she'd worry about being pregnant, and I didn't want her to worry about it.

Well, fortunately she didn't get pregnant, which would have really been a disaster for us. So we were lucky, and I just took my chances in telling her that I was protected when I wasn't, so she wouldn't worry.

Both males and females might also lie to avoid talking frankly about some area of sex that bothers them. For instance, Dick, the sales executive, described how one woman told him she had told one of her sexual partners that she used no birth control when she really did, in order to get him to use a condom. As Dick commented:

I   She told him what she did because it was more embarrassing for her to sound like she was accusing him of maybe having something. So her lie was a more diplomatic, gentler way of asking him to use something. Also, her lie was a way to avoid the AIDS issue, which no one wants to address or talk about. So it's much simpler for her to tell him that she doesn't have birth control and it's up to him, rather than get into the whole AIDS issue. Besides, if she did get into this subject, maybe she might get answers she doesn't want to know. Plus, many women tell me that most men are not truthful in discussing venereal disease or AIDS anyway. No one wants to know or admit it if he has it.

Other lies might be used to reassure the other person—usually the woman lying to the man—about his sexual performance. For instance, Dee reported that she and some of her friends had sometimes told men they were fantastic in bed when they were not—a common sexual lie, according to Dr. Cole, who told me:

I   One partner may try to show the other she is enjoying herself, because there is fear of hurting someone else's feelings by exposing the truth. That's why a woman may lie about whether she was having an orgasm—because she doesn't want to discourage the man into thinking that he's inept or that she is sexually unresponsive. So she might just pretend or create a scenario to make him think he's doing the right thing, when in fact, he's not exactly, though he may be on the right track.

A good lie? Cole didn't seem to think such lies were usually a good idea because she tries to encourage people to be honest while learning how to tell a partner the bad news about his or her performance in a gentle, constructive way that encouraged improvement. As Cole explained:

II   Sometimes it may be better to hold back or alter the truth a little, if a person is afraid he can't communicate in a way that is going to be taken well. But when possible it's better to be honest and tell the bad news in a gentle way. For example, if a woman doesn't feel the man is doing something she likes, she might say something like: "I really appreciate the effort you put into our sexual relationship, and there are just a few things that I need to have changed for it to be really fulfilling for me."
      In other words, the person who wants some change can acknowledge the other person's effort and care, and then explain that there are some future refinements that are needed to make it good or satisfying or ideal. I think that's better than setting up a deception that the person is doing everything right, so he thinks he's right on track when he isn't. That's why I encourage people to be honest about what they feel and need. Then they can inform their

partner so he or she can try to correct what's wrong, and
they are more likely to get what they want that way.

Lies in the Heat of Passion

There are also what might be called "the heat of passion" lies—lies
uttered during sex, when people may say all sorts of things. The
person may actually mean them, at least for the moment, but often
they are just a kind of romantic wish fulfillment or enticement for
the other person, not really meant sincerely, but part of the sexual
play.

All this can be fine when such talk is part of a shared fantasy and
both partners know the boundaries and don't take it too seriously.
For instance, partners in the throes of passion fantasize about going
off to live together on some wonderful island. Such talk can be used
for fun, and as part of the play, according to Susan Scott, a
relationships expert and author of the forthcoming book *Create the
Love of Your Life*. Yet, there can be a danger in this for some people
if they take this play for love, when it is really just sex, which can
happen because sex is very powerful and is often mistaken for love
by very vulnerable people. Also, this shared fantasy can become a
problem if one person is believing what the other person is
fantasizing and acts upon that lie. Misunderstandings and
disappointments can result.

A good example of this is the story that Judy, a teacher and
seminar leader, told me about a woman she knew who had been
having an affair with a married man for four years. During the
affair, in the heat of passion, so to speak, the man had spoken of
things they would do together and about the gifts he would give
her. He emphasized his intention again and again in what for him
was really a fantasy sparked by the heat of the moment.

She was lucky to come to this realization so she could face the
truth, disengage from the relationship, and get on with her life.
But not all people do this or escape the great pain of coming to
terms with reality, for as Scott commented: "People can sometimes get so caught up in the fantasy, that it hurts so much when
they have to face the truth. And there are some who may never
face that reality."

Lies about Seeing Others

Some dating couples may agree that it's okay to see others, but
many pledge mutual loyalty. Just as in a marriage, deceptions

may be used to maintain a monogamous ideal while one partner (or both) sees others.

For example, before he decided to change to a monogamous lifestyle, Dick, the sales executive, reported frequently seeing two or more women at one time, while denying it to them. As he told me: "There were several times where I was intimate with a couple of women at the same time, and they would ask me if I was sleeping with anybody else, and I would say no."

At times such denials can lead to uncomfortable confrontations. This happened when Alison, a counselor, decided she didn't believe her boyfriend John, who claimed he was going on a ski trip with male friends. She suspected that wasn't true and that he was really seeing another woman. She decided to check his story by waiting near his house and watching him leave. Soon, just as she suspected, the other woman showed up, and Alison decided to confront John. Needless to say, a raging, embarrassing argument ensued, with lots of yelling and tears. When John finally departed with his date, Alison felt devastated. Her relationship with John cooled quickly, and they soon broke up. She felt both vindicated and relieved at having exposed the lie, telling herself that it was better to be free of the "lying, deceiving bastard," however painful it was initially. Yet at the same time, she regretted the loss and felt upset and lonely for many months until she was able to find someone new. In the long run, she felt the exposure worth it, because she ended up with a very deep, committed relationship with someone she trusted fully and eventually married.

In the other cases, some dating situations turn into long-term stalemates in which there is a series of lies, confrontations, exposures, explanations, and still more lies. Why? Because the person lied to hesitates to let go of the relationship and comes to accept, tolerate, or avert her eyes to the cheating (and usually it is the woman who will try to overlook this), at least for a time. Meanwhile the person who's lying eventually lies again, since his partner doesn't want the truth and he wants to continue seeing others on the side. Susannah, the financial planner, had such an ongoing relationship with her on-again, off-again boyfriend Jerry. As she told me:

I   I got involved with Jerry because he swore to me he was interested in a serious relationship and really wanted to make it work. Well, we had gone together before, and we had broken up, because he kept seeing other women while telling me he wasn't going to do this. But now, he promised again he would be faithful.

And I thought he was. But then I happened to get a copy of this magazine that he publishes, and when I glanced through the personal ads, I saw an ad that I knew he had put in. He described himself just perfectly, and he even mentioned his new apartment with a view, which I had been helping him fix up.

Now I thought that was really outrageous. He was advertising for women on the one hand, and telling me that he's interested in a serious relationship with me on the other. So I confronted him about the ad and he admitted it was his. But then he insisted it was only for business reasons. Supposedly, he said, he wanted this ad to measure the response. Well, I told him, he could measure the response by counting the number of envelopes that come in for other people's ads. And he didn't really have an answer for that.

So afterward, we didn't see each other for a few weeks. We were supposed to go out that weekend, but I said no, and then I didn't hear from him for a while. But then he sent me a valentine, and I wrote him a note thanking him for it. And then he called me up and asked me out, and I said no. But after a while, he kept calling and I said yes again. So once again we've started seeing each other.

But the problem is still there, because he sees himself as an eternally available bachelor, while a part of him wants a permanent girlfriend. So he wants to have his cake and eat it, too, and he'll lie if necessary to do it. So do I call him on that or not? If I do, he just tries to deny it and maybe we'll fight. But if not, things just drift along as they are with Jerry's seeming commitment, though I know that's not really true. And I haven't decided which is better—what I have, which isn't really what I want, because I don't feel I can really trust Jerry, or no relationship at all.

Mixing Lies, Love, & Money

As in other sorts of relationships, lies about money in dating and intimate relationships sometimes come up. It is often those feelings of love, friendship, or trust that are used to nourish the lie, as happened three times to Frances, the computer-systems specialist.

In one case, a lawyer friend she dated told her he was going to file papers to incorporate a business, and she paid him to do this. But he took the money and never created the business. In another case, a man she had been seeing claimed that money was being wired to him in New York and said that if he could just get the money, about $1,000, for the plane trip to New York, he would pick up the money and come back. Though Frances explained that she was lending him her rent money and she desperately needed it back within a few days, he never repaid it. In fact, Frances lied herself in claiming this was rent money, because she did have a financial cushion and was using this claim as leverage to suggest how much she was sacrificing and risking to help. Even so, her occasional boyfriend didn't pay her back. And later, a third boyfriend took her for about $6,000 as a result of a series of loans that he promised to repay.

> But he never repaid me either. In fact, his last lie was to ask me for another loan of $2,000, claiming that if I didn't loan it to him, he wouldn't have enough money to make it through the month to be able to have the money to pay me back what he owed me from before. And I thought that was a bit much, so finally I said no.

Frances hurt even more because with him it hadn't just been a business venture; she had been in love.

This hurt and betrayal led Frances to hesitate to trust any male. Frances explained:

> I've just been afraid of getting involved again—with him, with anybody. For example, he's called me recently about trying to repay me. It was the middle of the night, and he announced that he was here and had about half the money. He told me: "If you'll see me tonight, I'll bring the $3,000. I've got $3,000 cash right here in my hand right now. And there don't have to be any strings attached. If I come to your door and I give you this $3,000 and if you decide that you don't want me in your place, that's all you have to tell me. And then I'll leave."
>
> But I didn't believe him. I just thought, with the door open, he could force his way in. Or maybe he didn't really have the money. Or maybe he'd just tease me

with it, promising to give it to me, but then he wouldn't. He'd find some excuse to hold it off.

So, what it came down to is that I didn't really trust him. So I said no. I said, "It doesn't feel right to see you right now," and I suggested that he call me for an appointment sometime during the day. He didn't call, so I think I was right not to trust him. I can't.

And I find I can't trust anyone else either. All of these situations have been so hard. I just feel like in the past I have had no control. I was like a wet rag. And so now I can't trust at all. I just say to myself "No, no, no." I feel I was hurt too much to trust again.

Lies in Fights

Arguments can be another time when lies come out and are used as weapons. Don, the engineer, described how he had experienced lies used as insults during fights with lovers. As he commented:

| Say you have a rift, a little misunderstanding with your primary person. I've sometimes had the experience of them saying things that aren't quite true just to throw a little barb at you. It's like they want to dig in their nails.

For example, a couple of times I have been trying to heal the rift and have been talking about meeting again, when all of a sudden the other person will say something like: "Well, are you really sure you want to meet again? I thought you didn't ever want to see me again." Well, it's like putting thoughts and feelings in your mouth, maybe because they're really worried that might be true, and they want you to deny it and reassure them. Or maybe they want you to imagine the possibility of never seeing them again so you are concerned it doesn't happen.

Anyway, for me, when this happens just before we say good-bye, it leaves me wondering and a little unnerved. I've been trying to patch up the quarrel, and then I start wondering "What's going on?" It's like having a rock thrown in some water that's just becoming calm, which starts stirring things up all over again.

Insulting digs, like direct hits, can hurt even more. Sarah, the educator, and one of her former boyfriends had been having an ongoing argument over their differing interests. While the fight had been patched over for a while, the raw feelings and resentments still simmered under the surface. As Sarah described it:

One of our problems was our differences. I'm normally a social person and I also like to dress up and go places at times, though I can wear jeans and do things informally, too. So being in the city is comfortable for me. But my boyfriend was often very uncomfortable in the city or with my social settings. And sometimes things got very tense because of this.

Well, this one night we went to a restaurant after going to the opera. And we had this incredible fight. I had really enjoyed the opera and I liked this restaurant, so I was in heaven. But my boyfriend, though I wasn't aware of this, was very uncomfortable. So all of a sudden, while I was really having a good time and feeling very, very good, my boyfriend suddenly lashed out at me and said that I was being just horrible. He claimed I was ignoring him, that I was making eyes at someone else, when I wasn't doing any of that at all. I think he was just making that up to start a fight, because he was feeling tense and irritable.

And then a few days later, he sent me a letter filled with lies and he told the counselor we were seeing that I didn't want to see the counselor anymore, when that wasn't true. Maybe he wanted to stop, but I didn't want to cancel the appointment. In fact, he even told the counselor I wanted to do this because I needed the extra hours and I was relieved that he canceled it for me. Which was also not true. Then, too, he sent a letter to the counselor, describing how I had been very angry that night and how he had tried to calm me down, when in fact I was the one who tried to calm him and stop the fight.

So he really misinterpreted everything. He tried to get me angry that night by what he said. And then he tried to get me angry again by sending me this untrue letter. I felt like he was like a child, trying to get me riled, maybe to get his own way or upset me because he felt he couldn't have what he wanted.

The Response to Lies

How do men and women respond to lies that sometimes pepper a relationship? At what point do the lies break up the relationship?

It would seem as if the occasional lie can be forgiven, particularly if the rest of the relationship is good and the lie is not serious.
It also depends on the individual who has been lied to. Some people
are more willing to forgive or see the lie as a reflection of the other
person's insecurity. So they decide it's not such a big deal. Others
may become incensed by lies about anything.

Some people are more ready to forgive. Why? Sexologist Louanne
Cole suggested it has to do with differing personality dynamics:

▎   Some people have a real sense of righteousness and
    justice, and they feel that being lied to is a major offense;
    while others are more tolerant. They take into
    consideration how big a lie it is. So if it's a big lie, then they
    would react against it more strongly. But if it's a minor lie,
    they wouldn't take it so seriously.
        And then there are those people for whom any lie
    undermines trust generally. They may feel if the person
    has lied about one thing then he may lie about others.
    They think: "If you could lie about that, then I don't know
    if I can trust you any more." And then, if they don't have
    an understanding of or an empathy for why the person
    lied in the first place, they may be closed to further
    understanding, and so it can be very hard for that trust
    to be rebuilt.

The response of the person lied to may depend on how the liar
responds. Commonly, lies come out not because the person recog-
nizes the lie at the time but because little things happen later to
reveal it, sometimes by illuminating discrepancies. Cole gave examples that come up in man-woman and dating situations:

▎   Other people or creditors call, and the other person
    picks up the phone and gets the gist of what is really
    going on. Checks bounce if there's a lie involving
    money. Or maybe families have disputes or family
    problems come to light, so the relationship turns out to
    be not what it seems. Or perhaps the weakness in the
    relationship is revealed when one person is in trouble,
    asks for help, and the other person doesn't respond. So
    various events can happen to bring the lie to light.

Once the lie comes out, people can respond in different ways
that make the lie easier or more difficult to accept. Sometimes the
response is denial, which, according to Cole, is especially com-

mon when there has been a liaison with someone else—"No, I wasn't really seeing someone else." Other liars accuse the victim of lying to get out of seeming to lie themselves. And then others, relieved to be caught lying, may actually confess. A person may explain the lies as something he or she did because "I didn't want to hurt you, and I thought if you knew, it would hurt. And so the better choice seemed to be to lie."

In any case, if the response to being caught in a lie works and the victim accepts or forgives, the relationship can continue. But it would seem as if this kind of repair work can only work so often—perhaps once or a few times, depending on how forgiving the other person is and whether the lie doesn't seem all that serious. However, if a pattern of lies builds up, that can lead to the end, as occurred for Dick, the sales executive, in one of his relationships. It happened with a woman he "really loved and could have been very happy with." As Dick described the breakup:

I   There were just too many things to accept so after a while I had to end it. For instance, when we first started dating, Judy called up and canceled a date with me at the last minute. She was supposed to come over to my place, but she said she couldn't be there because she was with a sick friend. Well, I knew she was breaking off a relationship with another guy to see me, and so I immediately suspected that she might have been with this guy. I wanted to know the truth, so I asked her not to be offended, but could I speak to the sick friend? But she said, no, because the sick friend was in bed. So then I asked if she would mind if I came over and talked to her in front of her sick friend's house because I needed to talk to her about something. But she said, no, you can't do that. And I asked why? But she had no reason. She just said you can't do that. So I felt that here she was probably lying.

But I just let that one pass, because I really did feel I loved her. But then another time, when we were supposed to go out of town together, I suddenly found out I had to go on a business trip the next Monday, so I said I couldn't go. Well, she claimed she could go with me, and I wondered how she could do this, because I knew she had all these customers. And she said she would just call them tomorrow to make other arrangements.

But she told me this on a Saturday morning, and I knew she couldn't really do this, because people don't work on Sunday and you can't reach them to reschedule appointments. That's not how business is done.

Then another time she said she was supposed to be speaking at an engagement, and when I said I would like to go hear her, she said she didn't want me to go because it would make her nervous. But I wondered about that because she is a professional speaker and she was going to be speaking to two hundred people. So how could I affect her that way? So finally she agreed that, yes, I could go. And I drove her to the engagement. But when we got there, she announced that she had gotten the wrong day, and she really wasn't speaking that day after all. And then she wouldn't let me speak to the woman who had supposedly booked her.

So I think she probably was never really ever scheduled to speak there. I think she just made the engagement up to impress me, because there was a big fair going on and there were going to be other speakers. And she just wanted to make it seem like she was going to be speaking too.

Anyway, though I loved her and thought she was a fantastic person in other ways, these little incidents began to build up and bother me. So finally I told her that. I told her how I loved her and thought she was great, and that I wasn't sure about what happened with the speaking or her sick friend and all that. But I wanted to ask her from this point forward to be sure to tell me the truth and that this is what I needed to continue the relationship. And she said fine.

But, as Dick related, she didn't do this, and finally one incident led to the end of their relationship. By itself, the incident might have been minor. But as a part of a pattern of lies, it was just too much. Dick described what happened:

I   Basically, the last straw occurred when we took a trip together. We drove to the country and we stopped in a restaurant. Then, suddenly, during dinner, she began to choke on some food, and the emergency medical people arrived and took her to the hospital for a little check-up. Then, while she was in the emergency room, I went through her purse to get her license so I could check her in, and I found that her license had a different age than what she had told me.

So later, after she left the hospital and we were driving home, I asked her how that could be. Well, she said that the DMV had made a mistake. So I said that I never heard of the DMV making a mistake on a person's birthday, or if they did, I thought it was pretty unusual for a woman to go along with letting her age be listed to show her as older than she really was—in this case four years older. But she insisted, no, this really was a mistake. So I asked her to do me a favor and get a new corrected license. But she said she couldn't, so I was sure this was just another lie. Had she told me she was four years older in the first place, it wouldn't have made any difference to me. And maybe if this was the only lie she had told me, it wouldn't have mattered. Just a little lie about her age.

But there were just so many lies before that for me this was the last straw. I loved her, but I just didn't want to deal with any more lies. And so for me, that was enough, and when we got home, I told her I wouldn't be seeing her anymore. The relationship was just over for me, and so that's how we broke up.

The Desire for & the Dangers of Honesty

As these stories show, the ideal is for honesty in the dating relationship, along with the goal of a greater intimacy—which is in turn premised on honesty and trust.

Yet, there is also a tension in achieving this goal in that part of the intrigue and excitement of the relationship comes from the mystery of the not fully revealed self. Raphael, the healer, made the distinction between being seductive in a relationship, which is okay, and being deceptive, which is not. The difference is in intent. In being seductive, one combines being warm, inviting, welcoming, open, and receptive with a kind of gentle and aware drawing in. But with deception, one holds something essential back.

But the paradox is that while this open honesty and giving of the self may sometimes cement the relationship through trust, at other times this openness may reveal too much that destroys the relationship. The reason is that the person who receives this truth is not always as tolerant as he or she may like to be. And that breeds a need to conceal.

Dick, the sales executive, described how he confronted this essential paradox:

> I realize that if you can say anything you want to, and the other person will still love you, then it is okay to be honest. That takes away a lot of the reason for lying because the fear of losing your relationship is gone.
>
> But can you really do that? I've had the experience of telling a woman that I want to be really honest, and then I asked if she's only seeing me now, hoping she will say yes and knowing that if she says no, it will turn me off. So I'm asking her to tell the truth. But if she tells me the truth I don't want to hear, I know that will end the relationship for me. I find it difficult to be receptive, forgiving, and accepting.
>
> So there's always that danger in being honest. It can destroy that very intimacy that it's designed to promote.

This is what happened to Sandy, the marketing consultant, when she told a man she had just met through an ad that she didn't feel any chemistry between them:

> This man had put an ad in a local singles paper, and as soon as I met him, I thought he was a basically nice, sweet person, but not right for me. I just thought we had very little in common, and I thought to save us the time and energy of trying to struggle through a conversation together over coffee, I would just tell him what I felt. So I told him that the chemistry was not right for me, though I thought him a nice person. And he seemed very insulted. So I've wondered since then about whether it's good to be so direct. It seems like some people just don't like to deal with the truth when it's so blunt.

Similarly, Roger, the philosophy teacher, seemed to feel as if he might have gone too far in trying to share his deepest, darkest secrets with a woman who encouraged him to open up and be more emotionally intimate. As he explained:

> I usually like to get everything out on the table, and if there's something standing in the way of me being con- nected with someone, I want to know what it is. Well, as it happened, I was seeing one woman, and we had a

great deal of sexual activity in our relationship. She complained that our relationship was just sexual and she wanted to share more emotional intimacy. So when she mentioned she had this diary she had been keeping for about seven years, I said I would like to read it, and she agreed as long as she could read mine.

So I gave it to her. But afterward, I wondered if this was such a good idea, because it contained my deep subjective feelings about what I do, and some of it is in X-rated language. Also, it included all the dates I had with this woman. So there were things there I didn't really want her to know about me. But I gave it to her, and I read hers.

And there were things in hers that I'm sure she really didn't want me to know about her, such as the fact she had had an abortion, and other things she had done. Afterward, I felt like we had maybe told each other too much. So this mutual revelation didn't really help the relationship. I think in our search for emotional intimacy we might have gone too far, because we both felt a little awkward about what we read.

And then she decided to go back to dating her former boyfriend, so our relationship ended anyway. But I think sharing too much helped to put a bit of a strain in it. So I guess I'm all for seeking that deeper intimacy. But at a certain point, you have to draw the line.

What complicates this ideal of honesty is the fact that women and men often have different ideas about how much should be shared and how much should be concealed for the relationship to be an honest one. Again and again, the individuals I interviewed and the therapists and business consultants I spoke to observed that women tend to reveal and want to have much more revealed. They reveal it to the men in their lives, and they reveal it to their friends and associates in talking about their men.

As speaker and author Judith Briles, who did several studies of male and female differences in the workplace,[2] commented to me:

Women are far more likely to divulge personal information to anybody. We women talk too much. We really share too much too soon. For example, at one group I spoke to, I remember saying:

"You know, I could sit down with any one of you, not knowing you, over a cup of coffee and within a very short period of time I would know about your love life, your married life, what kind of problems your kids have had, and what kind of female problems you have— information I'm not entitled to know."

Well, with that kind of orientation, the man may feel under pressure to talk about what he doesn't want to share. And the woman may perceive a lie (of concealment or denial) when the man does not. Perhaps as a counterbalance to this, women may also be more apt to suffer in silence at what they feel is a lack in the relationship, whereas men are more likely to act. As sexologist Louanne Cole observed: "Women sometimes tend to suffer a little bit more in the state of deprivation, whatever they're feeling deprived of, while the men will more often take matters into their own hands to do something and get what they want."

CHAPTER 9

Lies with Husbands, Wives, & Intimate Others

HEN IT COMES TO SPOUSES AND INTIMATE OTHERS, the ideal of honesty becomes even stronger, so that lies become even more frowned upon. Yet here, too, there are all sorts of lies, ranging from the common and usually harmless "You look great today, dear" lies to make the spouse feel good, to the lies that threaten the heart of the marriage because they are about affairs. Then, too, in a marriage or more intimate relationship, the lies bring up even more intensely that central puzzle of when it is best and most appropriate to lie to benefit the relationship—and when should the truth be told.

Stan, the high-school teacher, described a few of the lies he told his wife to promote her well-being, while pointing out that he considered their marriage to be based on a high degree of openness and mutual integrity. So why did he lie? In one case, to hide a doctor's verdict about her health problems from her so she would feel better; in other cases, to hold back a contrary opinion about things she had bought, to keep peace.

Such lies in a close relationship may be quite common and accepted, because their purpose is aligned with strengthening the relationship. Yet, despite the good intention, such lies may at times actually harm the relationship because they leave real thoughts and feelings unexpressed, and that can lead to misunderstandings and a build-up of resentment and anger.

Sexologist Dr. Louanne Cole pointed this out when she observed:

I   Sometimes lies can paper over unexpressed anger, such as when somebody asks what's wrong and the other person says: "Nothing," when in fact something is. I think it's important that people should get out their real feelings, because otherwise anger can build up and just fester, and then it will come out in some other way eventually.

So it's really important that people talk about what's bothering them or making them angry in a relationship, and they can do so in a way that is healing and releases the anger. They can do this by using "I" statements, in which they express the idea that "I think that . ." or "I'm feeling that . ." or "When you do this, it makes me feel this way . . ." or "When you do this, there's a consequence which is this and I don't like it." Such statements are designed to express the way the person feels and reacts to what the other person does, not blame the other person for those actions and reactions. So then the other person can be more receptive to listening and making a desired change.

However, if such concerns don't get expressed, this just messes up the relationship, because the anger will come out in one way or another—maybe in sex, maybe in money disputes, or in fights about how to raise the children.

In any case, the ideal is to be as honest and open as possible, since honesty is seen as the basis for true intimacy and commitment.

Alison, the relationships counselor, expressed this ideal quite intensely:

When I decided to get married again, I was real clear that I wanted somebody I could really trust. I knew I didn't want the uncertainty about trust to be an issue in my relationship, because I find that very draining, and I needed all my energy to put it into my work. So that was

really important on my list, and I feel my present husband has lived up to that completely. I feel I can trust
him in every way, and that's critical to me now.

Yet along with this ideal comes the problem of defining just
how honest partners should be—what should be revealed, what
should be concealed. It is not always an easy decision because with
openness comes vulnerability.

For example, Raphael, the healer, had gone through just such a
period of uncertainty and ambivalence during a very close
relationship with a woman he had considered a "significant other"
for about a year. As he told me:

I In our relationship, I think we were real honest with each
other, although there were certain concealments. But
were they really? Were they something that we should
reveal? For example, suppose something has happened
in the past, such as a previous extramarital affair or
extrarelational affair? When do you share that? In the
beginning? After the relationship has reached a certain
depth of intimacy and bonding? Or never?

It can be a drag if you always have to say everything
that's going on. I mean, there's a certain acceptance
that's needed, a certain respect for privacy, secrecy, and
autonomy of the other person. So how much should you
share? What's honest and what's not? When does that
line get crossed, indicating that you should share? How
is that defined? And then, if you should share, when is
the right time? It all can get very complicated. There's so
much that's uncertain and undefined, and you have to
develop your own definitions as you go.

Lies & Sex

The sexual relationship itself can be a big source of lies because it
involves such emotional intensity, and when people don't feel
comfortable about saying what they are really thinking and feeling,
they may prefer to lie. But again the paradox is that lying
sometimes can help the relationship by avoiding unpleasant truths
one partner doesn't want to hear. Yet at other times, lying can
interfere with the relationship by keeping one partner from getting
what he or she really wants because he or she doesn't ask for it or
says he or she wants something else (such as the classic case of the
woman feigning the orgasm).

Sexologist Dr. Louanne Cole pointed out such an example—a woman who had fantasies about the things she wanted her husband to do with her sexually, but she feared sharing these ideas with him. So she denied them, leaving her tense and in conflict. Finally, with therapy, she was able to open up and reveal them, resulting in an improved relationship.

As Cole told me:

I   This one woman was really upset about her sexual relationship with her husband, because she had some fantasies that involved him dominating and infantilizing her to make her feel like a little girl by embarrassing her and humiliating her. Somehow that turned her on. But she was very conflicted about the fact this turned her on, and she didn't want to reveal this to her husband. So she didn't talk about this.

But finally, after a lot of therapy, she was able to reveal some of this to her husband, and he had no trouble, it turned out, playing into this fantasy once he got the hang of what her script needed to look like. Also, he had no objections to doing this on ethical or moral grounds, just because her fantasy went outside the bounds of what might usually be considered normal. So in this case, it helped the relationship for her to be open and honest about what she really wanted.

Still, as Cole advised, it is important that people approach such revelations in a tentative way, much as the doctor I described in the previous chapter did in revealing his S&M desires to his girlfriends.

As Cole commented:

II   It's best when people do some what-if scenarios to see how their partner responds. Then they can watch how that person responds to other similar kinds of things in the news or on TV or in the movies or books. For example, when the movie *9 1/2 Weeks* came out, some women dragged their husbands off to see it because they had submissive desires, and they used the film as a testing ground to see if their husbands might want to put them in that role. Other people I know took their husbands to see that very erotic movie based on Milan Kundera's novel, *The Unbearable Lightness of Being*.

So people use movies frequently as testing grounds for some of their own desire. And some bring home porn films and books occasionally that reflect their own desires, and then they check on how the other person reacts to see if they can bring their own desires out in the open.

However, there are times such openness would not be helpful and could actually harm the relationship, so it might be better to lie. Some people need to keep certain areas of their life private and they need that space from their partner. In such cases, the denial or lie for concealment might be better than feeling a sense of personal invasion, which might undermine the relationship, too.

Cole described how some people have a need for pornography but must keep it secret from a spouse who might not approve. She felt in many cases it was quite justified for one spouse to have this separate part of his life to preserve his own sense of independence and privacy. As she commented:

I   Say a man wants to go to see pornography or explicit movies. Or maybe he might want to subscribe to *Playboy* magazine or see sexy films on the Playboy channel. But his wife or significant other might think this is just disgusting.

   Well, what sometimes causes problems in relationships is when people think that because they are married or in a very close relationship that they have a license to run the other person's life. They have this idea that they have a right to possess this other person, and they think they know how that person should best live up to their own potential based on their own ideals.

   But if the person didn't demand that, then a lot of lying wouldn't happen or be perceived as necessary, because what it can lead to is someone lying to avoid confronting the other person with the fact that a part of their life doesn't live up to the other person's idea of what their life should look like.

Ideally, of course, it would be preferable if the person insisting on this behavior could give up this insistence, so the lie would not be necessary.

I have found that some men choose to live double lives to hide their occasional participation in dominance-and-submission activities because their wives couldn't accept their taking a role that didn't fit their image of how he should be. If the man wanted to play a submissive scene or dress like a woman, he might conceal it from his partner but express it by going to some activity put on by some group in the D&S community. The men did not consider this to be the same as going to a prostitute or having an affair, since they experienced no sexual intercourse, just erotic arousal and release, and it seemed to work well for them.

Dr. Cole seemed to think this kind of double life might be appropriate for some. As she told me:

1   I think if people can tolerate that kind of double life and everything else is good about the relationship and this approach works for them and they don't absolutely need their own partner to be involved in the S&M or D&S scene with them, then that may be a choice that they should make rather than other choices, such as disrupting the family, breaking up the relationship, or revealing the variation that might bring about unnecessary embarrassments.

But then other people may want to come clean about their sexuality so badly that they can't tolerate any of that kind of subterfuge. So in that case, perhaps they should tell. They should be aware that the price may be high if they want to come clean, but if they need to do that, perhaps they should.

Likewise, there may be times when it is better to keep secrets or tell lies in the sexual relationship to make the other person feel better or maintain the sexual mystique. Louanne Cole pointed out that it might be best to keep it a secret when one's partner doesn't measure up to a physical ideal. As she put it:

I   I think there are better kept secrets, such as a woman's preference for penis size or a man's preference for breast size and that sort of thing. This is the case because a partner may have a preference for a particular size body part that seems important. But if he or she looks at the relationship as a whole and everything else about that relationship works very well, should he or she throw it all away because the partner doesn't have the ideal penis size or breast size that he or she is looking for?

Likewise, it may help to tell a little lie about what he or she thinks if the partner asks for an opinion about that part in the heat of passion. For example, suppose he says in the midst of passion: "How do you like my penis?" or something of that sort in more romantic terms. I don't think it's a terrible thing for her to say: "I think it's great, sweetheart." Or if she should ask him the same sort of question about her buttocks or her breasts, I think he should be similarly supportive, whether he thinks they're the greatest or not.

And the reason I think the lie is useful in such cases is because the person's body is not going to change. For the most part, there's nothing the person can do about his or her body, maybe just a few minor alterations here and there. So I don't think it serves the person to know that his or her partner has a critical feeling about such physical things or that they aren't really his or her ideal. Rather, I think it's better for the partner to be gentle and kind in saying what he or she thinks, so the partner feels better and that helps the person's self-esteem.

But if the partner was just being kind rather than saying what was true, would the other person really believe him or her? Cole didn't think this mattered, feeling that both would feel better through this shared romantic fantasy.

Other common fantasies are also better left unspoken. As Cole observed:

0   Sometimes people may think that if their partner fantasizes about other people, the partner doesn't love them, so that can encourage the lies such as: "I never fantasize during sex with you," or "I never look at other men." Or maybe he or she asks the partner: "What are you thinking about?" and he or she says "You," when in fact he or she is thinking about someone else.

Sometimes that can be a good response, because many people think that if one fantasizes about somebody, one really must feel that way or one will go and do it. But that is just not true. There are many, many fantasies that many people have that they have no intention of following through on.

Such fantasies may *be* about having sex with someone else, having a group-sex orgy, or a woman being forced to have sex. In the fantasy, this activity may seem like fun. But in real life these people would never go and do it or want such a thing to happen to them. The same goes for having fantasies about being dominated or embarrassed or humiliated in some way. There are some people who have such fantasies, but that's all they are. These things will never happen, and they don't want them to happen for real.

So sometimes if the other partner asks what you are thinking, it may be better to say "about you," or else not reveal the fantasy if it's not something the other person can understand or accept. Sometimes the other person has an idea of what he or she thinks the partner ought to be and won't budge from that position. So if he or she hears a fantasy that is different from that idea, they may think it bad or awful, which may hurt the relationship, and for no good reason, because the truth is just a fantasy. So for them I say, don't tell. It's better in such cases to keep the secret or deny.

And that's what many people do—lie about or deny their fantasies and feelings. Stephen, the writer, described what happened when his wife asked him to express feelings for her that he wasn't feeling at the time. As he told me:

Sometimes when Nancy asks me: "Do you love me?" and at that moment I'm not feeling love for her, I still say: "Of course, I do." That could be considered a lie, since I'm not feeling it at that moment. And there have been other times when I might say: "Yes, I love you," but I don't have any real conviction or passion about it right then.

And Nancy's reaction?

I   Sometimes she'll just accept what I've said whether she really believes me or not. It's not that big a deal to make an issue about it, and I've said what she's wanted to hear. But sometimes she'll call me on it by saying something like: "You're full of shit" or "You don't mean that." But generally that's as far as it will go. I'll just say something like: "Oh, sure I do," to keep the peace, or maybe I won't say anything at all. And then usually she'll let it drop and that will be the end of it, because neither of us really wants to pursue this, neither of us wants a fight.

Lying & Affairs

The lies with the most potential to do damage involve affairs or outside sexual liaisons, because these go to the heart of the marital or intimate relationship, which is usually based on the mutual monogamy. When such outside sexual relationships occur—and reportedly they do in about 30 to 50 percent or more of all marriages[1]—they usually are accompanied by lies designed to deny or cover up. The cheated-upon spouse may know or suspect, but may keep secret or deny his or her awareness to avoid bringing the affair out into the open, which might threaten the apparent calm of the marriage or relationship.

Such affairs occur for many reasons, ranging from a passing attraction to a way of coping with a marriage breakdown without breaking up the marriage. The affair can be beneficial by providing an outside release, although it also can create distance between the partners. Meanwhile, the lies about the affair become another layer in the mix.

Don, the engineer, described his own ambivalent feelings about having the relationship and lying about it:

)   Lying in a monogamous relationship is not an acceptable lie to me, although I admit that sometimes in the past I have done this. And then I have felt guilty about doing it. I just feel it's an essential dishonesty to the relationship.

Why, if so many couples have extramarital or extra-significant-other relationships, do they not admit it and work out ground rules? According to Susan Scott, the expert on relationships and author of the forthcoming *Create the Love of Your Life*, the reason many do not do this is because of the power of the monogamy-fidelity ideal. As she observed:

Sometimes people have open relationships. But most of the time the spouse is never told, because the person having the affairs knows it will never be okay with that spouse, and they fear the loss of the spouse, even though they may be unfulfilled at home. So even though they are still unhappy, they want to hold onto the relationship, and fear disrupting it by telling and admitting they have violated this monogamous ideal.

Also, a person may conceal a past affair to maintain his own image of purity or integrity and to prevent the other person from feeling hurt, again because of this monogamy ideal. Joyce, a personnel counselor, described how she kept secret a past affair with an accountant because she didn't want to worry her husband. As she told me:

I   My husband and I have an extremely open and intimate relationship with each other. It's completely monogamous and based on an ideal of sharing everything with each other.

But there is one thing I never told my husband about and that's that I had a sexual affair with one man who is still our accountant. He was my accountant as well as my lover before our marriage, before I divorced my previous husband. And after our affair was over, I still wanted to use him as an accountant because he is very good.

So I never told my husband about the affair. It feels like a lie to me not to tell him, because we are so honest and open about everything else. But I can't see any reason to tell him. If I did, I think he would just feel uncomfortable with this man and wonder about the relationship in the past or worry about it happening again where there's nothing there and won't be again.

Although this lying and secrecy associated with current or past affairs can produce feelings of guilt for many people, for many others this lying and secrecy are part of the excitement of the affair. Doing something forbidden heightens the sense of romance and physical passion. And for some people feelings of excitement and guilt along with fears of being found out are interwoven, alternately drawing the person more intensely into the affair or making him or her reconsider it.

In some cases, of course, guilt can lead a person to stop the deceptions by finding an alternate outlet, such as becoming busy. Some common ways of doing this might be by volunteering for something, becoming more active in one's business, or even cleaning up the house, according to Scott. For example, Judy, the teacher and seminar leader, told me about a friend who couldn't stand the deception after he cheated on his wife with a one-night stand, so he threw himself into community work to escape a marriage that was going downhill. He couldn't handle the guilt and secrecy of an affair.

Other people who feel guilt usually work through it by rationalizing or saying that the benefits of the affair are well worth it.

And many people find ways to compensate for their guilt, such as the man who buys an extra nice present for his wife because he is cheating on her. Still others channel their guilt into being supersensitive about discovery, and they become extra cautious to keep their secret.

Types of Concealments & Justifications

How do people who have affairs conceal them? Some use fake excuses and explanations such as "I have to work," "I have to go out of town," and the like. But as the outside relationship goes on, the person may have to come up with more believable reasons, particularly if there is a change in the person's situation that makes the outside relationship more difficult to carry on.

Scott pointed out that concealment strategies can lead to difficulties because the cheating partner may lead what becomes a double life. For instance, Annie, a communications consultant, described a friend whose husband was fairly successful in keeping an outside jogging-sexual relationship carefully hidden.

I   This one man I know has a woman friend he jogs with two or three times a week. They also take time out to have sex together. And sometimes they go off on runs together, which take them away for a weekend or so. And they have been enjoying this relationship with each other for a couple of years.

But at the same time, he has had to maintain the lies with his wife and lead a double life.

And ironically, what's fascinating is that the two people who are affairing are often more honest with each other than they are with their spouses, because they aren't responsible for each other's overall well-being.

For example, the man doesn't have to worry about being Mr. Macho and taking care of the woman, because she is being taken care of someplace else. So he can be more himself and allow himself to be more vulnerable and therefore more honest. It's not likely that this kind of outside relationship will lead to marriage, since most people in affairs stay with their mate. And they use the lies and the cover-ups with their primary partner to help maintain this dual state of affairs.

Some couples may also use their friends to help them maintain their cover-up. A classic example of this is when a person having an affair gets a friend to open up his or her home, so the couples can have a supposedly safe place to go. But more generally, in the interest of secrecy, friends will be kept out of this. One reason is that many people having affairs don't want even their friends to know, because their friends may disapprove or that knowledge provides one more loose link that could lead to exposure. Then, too, it may not be a very good idea to involve friends in actively protecting the affair, because if the affair comes out, they might be targeted by an angry mate.

Such lies can work for a long time, because the other partner wants to believe and trust, and even may try to screen out any potential suspicions.

Then, too, the people lying can often be quite convincing, especially when they can push away feelings of guilt and compartmentalize their lives, so that leading the double life causes no qualms.

While there is much uncertainty about male and female differences in their success in managing the affair, the popular view appears to be that men have an easier time of doing this, since they are better able to compartmentalize their lives—say by having a wife at home and a lover at work or putting lust in one category and love in another. This may be because some men tend to be more in control of their emotions, or at least don't express their emotions so openly, because from early childhood males are taught to show control and not express emotions. Thus, when having the affair, such men may feel or express their feelings less openly, because their emotions are more underground. As a result, they are better able to conceal their feelings for the other women or any effect of this on their relationship with their married or primary partner.

By contrast, because many women may be more apt to experience or express their emotions openly, women may be more apt to act in a way that triggers their partner's suspicion. But then, whether there are these male or female differences or not, those married people who have successful affairs are those who have learned how to be more in charge of their emotions to maintain concealment. As Scott commented: "Those that are able to compartmentalize have a strong survival motivation to keep the affair going by keeping it secret, and they do this for that reason."

Of course, some lies unravel, and the secret comes out. In some cases this happens because the partner has just gone too far in trying to invent and create, so the lie sinks of its own weight.

Blanche, the public-relations executive, described a situation with her first husband, who had gotten his mistress pregnant and then let the cat out of the bag, so to speak, when he tried to figure out what to do about it. As Blanche described it:

I I was in my early thirties, married to my first husband, and one day he asked me for the name of a girlfriend of mine who is a nurse, and then he called her and asked her for the name of a doctor who would do an abortion for a co-worker of his.

Well, my friend came to me and said that this was a funny thing for my husband to ask her, and she suggested: "I bet he's knocked up someone in his office." At first, I said: "Oh, that's impossible," and I just thought her idea was funny.

But then, her suggestion acted as a kind of a trigger, and I soon put two and two together when one of his partners at a social engagement said how much time my husband was spending with one of his co-workers at a luncheon counter. It was the same woman he had asked about the abortion for, and so I became suspicious, and when I confronted him about it, he admitted it was so, and that helped me realize that our marriage had been going along, not being very good. And so, though the incident and the lie weren't the cause, they really served as the beginning of the end of our marriage, and we soon got our divorce after that.

While the revelation of a lie may lead to the end of the relationship in some cases, it may lead to further concealments and lies in others, building a foundation of lies.

A good example of this is the wife one interviewee told me about who uncovered her husband's affair and made him call his mistress and tell her the affair was over while she listened. But in fact, he called the mistress back later and the affair went on, though now the partners worked even harder at keeping it secret. They changed their meeting places and times; they set up signals to use in calling each other, so each would know when it was safe to take the call. Also, they paid more attention to small details, and generally became even closer to each other.

This greater intensity in an affair may in turn result from this greater fear of exposure, according to Scott, because this fear and the added concealment efforts can strengthen the power of the affair. Why? "Because," Scott commented, "different things turn people on. For some people, the taboo of the forbidden is more exciting. It acts like an aphrodisiac to make the affair more intense and stronger, though for other people that same fear can kill the relationship."

Revealing & Reaction to the Lie

Sometimes, even with all these efforts to conceal, the lie is revealed. Often a mistake, some sort of chance happening, brings the secret out, although according to Scott, there may be other clues, which the other person may be able to pick up, if he or she is ready to see them, even though these clues can be quite subtle. As Scott commented:

> When someone is really close and tuned into someone else, he or she will always be able to see the truth. Although if someone isn't ready, he or she will miss it, because he doesn't want to see what's there. This is so, because if you use your intuition, you will always see the truth.
>
> For example, some of the clues a person might see might be clues given off by the sense of touch, taste, or smell. There could be visual clues in the way the person acts; sound clues in the way the person says something. Some examples of this might be one partner acting nervous or not looking into the other person's eyes. Also, perhaps out of guilt or as a way of making up for having the affair, the person may become unusually nice or thoughtful, such as bringing flowers or an extra present, that seems unexpected or inappropriate.
>
> However, whether the spouse experiencing this recognizes these differences is another issue. The spouse may not always do so, because he or she may not want to see what is happening, so it is easier to lie to oneself. But these differences, these clues to the truth are there.

One reason for not wanting to acknowledge is, of course, the underlying betrayal and shock to the self-esteem such involvement with another may bring. But another reason is that in facing the situation, the person will have to do something about it, and may not want to face the pain of taking this action. A wife, Scott observed, might have to confront her husband, which frightens her, because it would shake up the marriage. Also, she might be called on to make decisions about the marriage that she doesn't want to make, and she might lose everything. Thus, by maintaining a state of denial, she can keep what she thinks she has in the relationship.

In other cases, the spouse really may not be aware, because he or she hasn't been paying attention or the clues have been too subtle. But then, all of a sudden, their spouse does something that gives the affair away, and all of the clues become apparent.

Due to traditional roles and upbringing, the wife may be slower to suspect and the husband quicker to become aware earlier, because he is more likely to be jealous or possessive and so be on the alert for such clues. But, regardless of gender, Scott feels that the person who wants to hold onto the illusion the most is the last to suspect, and one cannot generalize about whether men or women are more likely to do this, because roles and situations today vary so greatly.

Another traditional pattern that still seems to be common is that when men do find out, they tend to be more angry, hurt, and violent than women, and they are less ready to adjust, accept, and forgive, perhaps because of this tendency to be more jealous, possessive, and ego-involved. At least the high level of statistics on wife abuse and male violence against ex-wives or wives who have tried to leave seems to bear this out. Then, too, men may be more apt to express their hurt outwardly through action, rather than release the pain by talking about it, as is more common for women who may find more support from others in sharing their grief. Yet, again, such patterns may be changing, as men increasingly learn to get in touch with their feelings today, and in Scott's view, those who are better able to express emotion will be less apt to express it in angry, violent ways, and better able to adjust, accept, or forgive.

So what happens when the spouse finally finds out or admits that he or she knows? The spouse might continue to deny it openly, hoping the affair will go away without a confrontation. So in this case there can be a collusion in which the spouse, usually the wife, decides not to make an issue of it, to keep the relationship as it is. Such a person might be feeling a great deal of emotional pain, according to Scott. But he or she just doesn't want to risk the possibly greater pain of losing the relationship he or she has. But then, when the person does finally find out or acknowledges what is really going on, Scott feels it will help the person to break free and move on.

A woman in this situation, according to Scott, might be able to rationalize that as long as her husband pays the bills, takes her on nice vacations, and otherwise treats her well, she doesn't want to rock the boat. She might overlook the situation. But, according to Scott, when a person is settling for less than what he or she really wants, that person won't be really happy, because they won't truly respect themselves.

On the other hand, some people who do bring everything out in the open can be quite devastated on the surface, leading to all sorts of reactions—from tearful discussions to angry confrontations to wives or husbands hiring private detectives to confirm their worst fears and finally to divorce.

When Dee, the real-estate investor, suspected her husband was cheating on her, she started playing detective.

> I hated lying to my husband. But I felt I had to because I thought he was lying to me. So I tried calling his office or calling him when he was home, and then when he answered, I would hang up, because I just wanted to know if he was there. When he asked me sometimes about this the next day, asking me, "Did you try to call?" I would just say no. Though I'm not sure if he believed me either. So things started to get quite uncomfortable.

Eventually, as their relationship deteriorated, the affairs started to come out into the open. Her husband didn't seem to care whether she knew, so there was no more need to lie. She even saw some of his women come to the house, and finally he moved out entirely. The marriage was over, and so were the lies.

In other cases, marriages have been healed after a period of upset and turmoil following the revelation of the lie. Louanne Cole pointed out how this had occurred with one of her clients.

He had been having an affair because he needed variety in his sexual partners after twenty years of being married to one woman, who started to devalue the importance of sex in their relationship. However, he didn't want to disturb the marriage. But eventually, the affair was revealed when the husband of the other woman he was seeing became suspicious, taped a phone conversation between the lovers, and then played it to the wife.

One result of this was that the woman herself went through a period of renewed sexual activity with him to show him that she could do it. Then, proving herself and arousing his interest again, she pulled away. So it was her way of making him feel bad about what he had done. But then, gradually, with extended therapy, they have been repatching their twenty-year marriage, in part because she was motivated to stay married to him for financial reasons.

In other cases, the revelation of the affair might in the long term actually be very healing for the original relationship. The result might seem paradoxical, but, as Scott observed, sometimes this can renew the partner's sexual interest in each other. As she observed:

> The revelation of the affair can act like a wake-up call on not taking each other for granted any more. Also the feelings of jealousy can show the partners that they really care about each other.
>
> So the revelation can be used in a positive way if people really have a good intention to make the relationship work again, although this kind of result is rare. Generally, people don't have the skills to deal with this situation. But if they can, then the discovery of the affair can act as a turning point to shake up the marriage, since trauma can lead to positive change. So possibly it could lead them to correct the problems in their relationship and move on to a better relationship and companionship, much deeper and much stronger than before. Though it will take work in dealing with the issues in the relationship to get to this point.

Lies to the Other Man or the Other Woman

While such lies to the spouse are an inherent part of the secrecy and intrigue involved in any affair, very often there are lies to the other man or woman as well. Although the partners in an affair may be more honest with each other, because they have no formal responsibilities to each other or public images of a marital relationship to maintain, in many other cases their relationship is shrouded in lies.

One big lie, of course, is that the other person isn't married or is planning to get a divorce. When the partner in the affair finds out the truth, it can be devastating.

Blanche, the public-relations executive, described having this experience several times when she had an affair. As she told me:

> The first time I discovered this man I was seeing was lying to me, it was terrible. I had just graduated from

high school, and I was dating this very tall, handsome medical student who was a basketball player, and I was very much in love. I thought everything was dandy. We had spoken about marriage.

And then one day I got a call from this woman who told me she was married to him and was having his baby. I was shocked. I couldn't believe it. Here is this man who was two-timing the woman he was married to while she was about to have his baby, and he was two-timing me, too.

I felt so hurt, and I cried and cried. It was so hard to break up with him, but of course, I did. I couldn't go on with the situation after that.

In a situation involving another man, she discovered the truth when she went to his apartment after several broken dates.

I   I wanted to see him to find out what was going on, so one night, I went to his apartment and sat outside until two in the morning. I just waited. And when he didn't come, I realized he was out all night. So I went home and about ten in the morning I called him on it. Well, he tried to cover his tracks and give some excuse why he was so late.

But I knew. I knew he had been cheating on his wife to be with me, but he had explained that was because he didn't love her and they just had this marriage of convenience. But now he was cheating on me, though I had come to expect him to be faithful. So it hurt me a lot, and after that I tried to work on finding him unattractive. If I couldn't have him completely outside of his relationship with his wife, I decided it was time to get him out of my life.

Lies When the Marriage Ends

Lies often come up in the marital relationship at the bitter end. Two types of lies are common—those used to get back at the ex-or soon-to-be-ex-spouse; and those used to get more money.

Revenge lies express anger. Dick, the sales executive, described how one of his divorced friends told lies about his ex-wife to smear her reputation out of bitterness. As Dick commented:

I   He just wanted to hurt her. For instance, one time I went to a class reunion, and he and his ex-wife were both there, because they had gone to that school together. Well, he was going around telling everybody there that they should go get into her pants, because she was so easy. And that was a lie. He was really libeling and disparaging her, because he had lost her, so he wanted to put her down.

After her own divorce, Sarah, the educator, discovered that her former husband was lying about her to their children, now living with him and his new wife.

/ He was just saying awful things about me, telling them I didn't really care about them, that I was being promiscuous with other people, things like that. He was really blowing things about me totally out of proportion.

So finally I called his wife and told her about this, and then I spoke to him. I told him: "I don't say things about you, and if the kids say anything disparaging about you, I try to help them see things from your point of view. So why are you doing this? Why do you feel you have a need to say bad things about me?"

Well after that, he didn't have much to say, and I thought I had made peace with him about this. But later, as the kids were growing up, I found out he was still doing this. I thought I had smoothed things over and we were friends again. But apparently we weren't. He was still feeling very angry about what happened, and I think his lies about me were his way to get this out.

As for the lies to get more money, some partners may simply do this out of greed, others because they feel their partner is not being fair to them, and the lie is their way of fighting back. This is what happened when Alison was going through what she described as "a really nasty" divorce. Her husband was "hateful and vengeful," and he was trying to give her as little as possible from the business they shared. So she used her own bluff to get him to give her a loan to buy a house she wanted. As Alison told me:

I When my husband and I were married, we owned a small manufacturing company. And since I was the book-keeper, as well as one of the co-owners, I knew what the business was worth—almost a million dollars. In fact, we had started with most of my money.

Then, when we got divorced, he was very unhappy and spiteful about this, and he tried to give me as little as he could. So he lied, claiming the business was only worth $200,000, and he had phony books, though I knew it was worth closer to $800,000.

However, I had the kid. He was just about four at the time, and my ex was worried that I was going to move out of the area and take the kid with me. So when I found out he was worried, I decided to use this information against him. This happened when I decided to buy a house, and I found I needed $25,000 for the down payment. I had ended up with a much smaller settlement than I should have gotten, only about $100,000, instead of $400,000, because of the way he lied. So I didn't have enough for the house, and I asked him for this extra amount. But he wasn't going to give it to me.

Well, that's when I decided to lie myself. So I told him that I wanted this money, and that all he had to do was to take a loan from the bank against the business, which would be easy for him to do. And I told him that if I didn't get this money to buy this house, I was moving. Well, I was bluffing.

But he bought my bluff, and so I got the money to put down to buy the house. And now it's worth three times what I paid for it, so that way I almost got back what he cheated me out of.

And then the business he cheated me out of got demolished in the recent San Francisco earthquake, so I feel that's a kind of karma or justification for what he did to me, too.

Usually, I don't like to lie. It's always been very important to me to be totally honest with people. But in this case, I feel proud of getting away with that lie to get the house. It felt so justified to do that because that was my only trump card. That lie was the only thing that I had to get a piece of what was mine.

And then, too, the lie was also for my son, because I wanted him to grow up in a nice neighborhood. So, yes, I'm quite proud of that lie and getting away with it.

CHAPTER 10

The Lies of Parents & Children

PARENT-CHILD RELATIONSHIPS ARE PEPPERED WITH LIES. Likewise, children lie to each other, and the lies become more complex as they grow up. Commonly, children are taught very early not to tell a lie, and it's part of the tradition of religion and morality passed down from parent to child. Yet very young children begin to lie as well, sometimes because they experience lies from their parents and other adults or older children. Then too, children soon discover the benefits of lying for much the same reason that adults do—to impress others, to avoid punishment or disapproval, to get out of something they don't want to do.

What Parents Tell Children about Lying

The ideal of honesty has a long history, wrapped in notions of traditional morality and religion, with admonitions against lying derived from the Judo-Christian tradition and from other religions. And there are all sorts of outside supports for this idea as well. For example, traditional stories such as *Pinocchio,* about the little boy whose nose grows long when he tells a lie, support the notion that the lie will be discovered and punished. Religious leaders convey this message, too—it's wrong to lie.

The people I spoke with pointed out how they had been given this message early: Don't lie; it's wrong to lie; the lie will be revealed. For example, Alison, the relationship counselor, said:

II   My parents made me afraid to lie. I don't remember specifically, but they led me to believe that something bad would come back and get me or something bad would happen. Somehow the lie would haunt me.

Don, the engineer, stated:

0   I recall my parents telling me I wasn't supposed to lie and my mother could tell by looking in my eyes if I was doing this. She really couldn't, but she claimed she could.

For Storm, the writer, there was always the threat of hell if the lie was serious enough.

I   They told me that lying was a sin, but if it was just a simple lie, I wouldn't go to hell. Instead, there would be purgatory, though it would have fire and damnation, but one could get out of it someday. But then, for a really serious lie, there might be no possibility. So I had that drilled into me when I was a child—lying was a sin, with the appropriate punishments for the lie.

While this message of "don't lie" may come through loud and clear, children very often may get a double message when they discover that their own parents lie.

Susannah, the financial planner, described this confusion:

I remember my parents telling me how it was wrong to lie, and they used stories to illustrate their point, such as the story of George Washington and the cherry tree.

But then, even though they expressed this ideal, they behaved differently. For instance, my mother lied all the time, and my older sister did, too. So perhaps that's why I tried to become exactly the opposite as I grew up. I thought what they were doing was so hypocritical and wrong.

When Parents Lie

When do parents lie? Very often it's to guard their children by concealing information or opinions to protect their feelings or to keep inappropriate information from them. Then, too, parents may want to keep back painful information, such as a family secret, or conceal their disapproval. Or they may lie simply to get their kids to do something. Parents commonly justify their lies to children as being in the best interests of their kids, although again and again, the people I spoke to told me that however painful, they really would prefer to know the truth.

Lies to Protect Feelings

Parents may lie to protect their kids' feelings by telling them they are doing something better than they really are or by not sharing a negative opinion. The goal is to help their kids feel better about themselves and build self-esteem, and the parents I spoke to felt quite justified in doing this. After all, these were helpful, benevolent lies.

Stan, the high-school teacher, described how he did this with his daughter.

> **I** I'm not always absolutely truthful with my kids, particularly my daughter. She is really very competent, and I get angry sometimes that she doesn't do more academically than she can. But I try to keep that back. For instance, one time she said: "You know, I only made a C," and I said: "Well, that's all right. You did the best you can." But I know that was a kind of a lie, because I really think she should be getting a B, because I know she could do it if she tried.

Stan continued:

> **II** I told her the lie because she's easily discouraged. She has two academic parents and a super-bright genius brother, and that's really hard on her.
>
> Thus, though she is perfectly competent and could do better, she has decided that there's nothing wrong with a C, which is average. She feels more comfortable thinking of herself as average, so she doesn't have to feel she is competing with others in the family. She

really is above average because she tests above average, and she could be above average if she wanted to.
But much of the time she doesn't, and so her mother
and I try not to press that because it just makes it
worse. We just let her think we think what she is doing
is okay, though really we think it's not.

Lies to Conceal Opinions or Disapproval to Avoid Undue Influence

Sometimes parents lie, particularly as children get older, to conceal their opinions or disapproval of certain behavior to avoid a
conflict or to influence their kids in a choice they feel the kids
should make themselves. While some children might appreciate
the freedom from parental opinions, others felt a sense of distance at not knowing what their parents thought.

Stephen, the writer, commented:

My parents often wouldn't tell me the truth or share their
ideas about how they felt about what I was doing or what I
had done or who I was living with or that sort of thing.
They just seemed to find it difficult to tell me what they
thought or share their feelings. I think it's because they
wanted to keep the peace. They didn't want to rock the
boat or get me upset if we had different ideas about
something. But I really would have liked to know.

Lies to Conceal Inappropriate Information

Parents also may lie to keep their children from knowing something they think he or she shouldn't. This can be something that
puts the parents or the family in a bad light; at other times they
just feel the children are too young or this is inappropriate information for them.

With very young children, the Santa Claus or Easter Bunny tales
fall into this category. Parents want their children to believe in this
kind of childhood fantasy, and they don't want to be the ones to
break the bubble of childhood innocence.

On a more serious note, parents may conceal the reality of death
from their children. Alison, the counselor, recalled that her first
experience of being lied to occurred when she was four years old
and her grandmother died.

II   But nobody told me. My parents just kept me in the
      dark. They just gave me excuses about why I couldn't
      see my grandmother, why she couldn't come to visit.
      And I didn't find out until years later about what really
      occurred.

Did Alison believe the lie to be a good one? "I felt like they were
keeping something from me, and I felt helpless, like I didn't have
any control."

Another such example occurred for Raphael, the healer, when
his parents tried to conceal their experience of the Holocaust. His
father had gone through the horrors of the concentration camp,
and Raphael seemed to think that his parents should have told him
about this so he could better understand his own background and
heritage. But they held it back to protect him, as well as
themselves, from the memories of such suffering.

Still other concealment lies concern the parents' sexuality, particularly when the children are young. Parents just don't want the
children to know about this, and may feel uncomfortable talking
about sex generally as well. So the lie or denial becomes a handy
way of covering up.

Frances described how her own parents used these gentle lies.

I/   When I was a kid I remember that my parents always
      lied about this. For example, they would say they were
      so tired that they had to go to bed at 8 o'clock when I
      was a little kid. But later in life, you learn that there's
      more in bed than that you're dead-tired at 8 o'clock.

Joyce, a therapist and mother I spoke with, felt it appropriate to
disguise or evade to avoid giving young children inappropriate
sexual information, using her own experience with her three-and
five-year-old daughters as an example. As she commented:

0   I basically regard myself as an honest person, but
I've used disguise or evasion with my young daughters to
keep information I think is inappropriate from them. For
instance, say I am in a public lavatory with my daughter,
and she says: "Oh, is this where they put the diapers?" I'll
say: "Yes, it's for babies' diapers," even though it's used
      for something else, for used tampons, because I don't
think it's timely for her to know this. There will be a time
when I will tell her all about the subject, but at age three
                          or five, I don't think it's appropriate.

Another example might be explaining other inappropriate or taboo subjects, such as where babies come
from. I'm not going to get involved in some long and
complicated explanation of sex at this point. It's not
something a child of that age needs to know. So I might
say something quite honest, such as the baby is pushed
out from "down there." But I wouldn't go into any big
explanation about the mechanism of what happens. So
instead, rather than do this, I might evade or disguise or
tell white lies. I try to give out the appropriate information
and be honest about that. But beyond that I think it's
appropriate to lie and evade.

Lies to Get a Child to Do Something or Not Do Something

Finally, another big category of parent lies is made up of those little
lies they tell to get their child to do or not do something. For
parents, such lies may seem like clever tricks to help shape desired
behavior, but they can seem quite hurtful for the child, as well as
providing a model of deceit for the child.

Sandra, the marketing consultant, ended up going to the college
her parents wanted her to attend because of the way her parents
used deception to guide her choice. Later this recognition
contributed to her growing distance from them. As she explained:

I   When I was young, I always had this fascination with
the West. There was something about its old mystique,
the myth of the frontier, the romance of the cowboy, the
image of the old farmstead, that helped to intrigue me,
even though all this was long past in the modern day.
Also, I had long listened to country-and-western hits on
the radio; so in many ways I felt this connection with the
West.

Thus, when it was time to go to college, I wanted to
go to a western college, though we lived on the East
coast. And my parents actually did take me visiting to
many colleges in the Midwest, as well as to schools in
New England and New York.

In the end, there was a school I decided I wanted to
go to in Minnesota, because when we were there I had
really liked hearing stories about the early frontier days

there. It had many stories about the escapades of the old outlaws, and I loved the countryside, too.

But I also won a scholarship to a school in the East, and my parents really wanted me to go there, because they would save some money. So they worked on convincing me. And one of the arguments they used was that this was really a western college, because it was so close to Ohio. So they played upon my old fantasies and my lack of real knowledge of U.S. geography to finally convince me.

And I did go there, though I always felt like it was the wrong choice, like I didn't belong. And for a long time after that, I resented my parents for tricking me into making this choice, because they really wanted me near to them and wanted to save the money. Eventually, I hated it so much that I finally ended up leaving and breaking away to go to California. And that helped me break away from my parents, too.

When Children Lie

Whether children learn it from their parents or do it for other reasons, they learn to lie very early. According tp psychologist Paul Ekman, author of *Why Kids Lie'* and numerous articles about children and lying, by the age of four, or even earlier, "children can and will lie—not simply making excuses or confusing fantasy with reality, but deliberately attempt to mislead."[2] According to Ekman, the usual reason is to avoid punishment, commonly by claiming "I didn't do it."

Initially, parents may have this notion of childhood innocence. They may think of their young children as "sweet innocents, uncorrupted speakers of pure truth," and they like to think their own children wouldn't lie or try to deceive them, according to Ekman.[3] But the truth is that children discover sooner than parents think that they can get away with their lies at least some of the time, and as they get older they get better and better at it at the same time that they become better at detecting lies. They learn to control the sound of their voices and the looks on their faces and avoid the obvious inconsistencies or obviously untrue alibis, and they also tend to feel less guilt about lying, particularly by the time they reach adolescence. One reason that guilt may subside, despite the early admonitions against lying, is that children simply get used to lying more; they become desensitized to it and increasingly discover that others around them, regardless of any moral principles against lying, are lying, too. Then, too, the decline in guilt may be related to the rejection of parental values that comes in adolescence. As Ekman suggests:

> One reason adolescents are more successful liars is that they feel less guilt about lying to their parents or teachers. Rejecting parental values—noticing the clay feet that authority stands upon—is a common form of rebellion. For some teenagers, lying may be one way of establishing their own identity, of achieving independence—a necessary task of adolescence.[4]

Lies to Escape Punishment

The people I spoke to recalled plenty of examples of the lies they told when young to try to avoid making their parents angry or escape being punished when they knew they had done wrong. Usually they were caught, because they weren't very good at lying, or they felt bad, because they still were impressed with the traditional childhood admonition that lying is wrong.

Stephen, the writer, recalled taking a music box from his mother when he was about four or five and then denying that he took it.

> I didn't really steal it. I just really liked it and I took it. Then I was caught and punished. I tried to deny that I took it, but my mother didn't believe me, and punished me. I'm not sure if that was for lying or for taking the box.

In Sarah the educator's case, the crime was taking candy from a store, though eventually she felt so guilty that she finally admitted what she did.

> I was about six or seven, and at first I acted like nothing had happened. But then I started to feel so guilty that I told my mom. Then she had her boyfriend take me and her back to the store so I could confess what I did. I felt relieved when I did it, but it was also a horrible feeling, too, because I felt like such a criminal for what I did.

Many times these lies were caught, but in many other cases they were not, often because the parents did not want to think their child had lied.

For example, Dick, the sales executive, described how he got away with many lies because his parents thought of him as a "good" boy.

> So they didn't catch me when I lied about all kinds of things. For example, they would tell me to stay home, and I would go away, and then I would tell them I stayed home. Or they would ask me who broke a window, and I would tell them somebody else broke it, though I did, and other things like that to escape punishment.
>
> But they tended to believe me, because they had instilled in me the idea that it's wrong to lie, that lying is a sin, and you had to confess it. Well, I would confess it, and I did feel better after that. Also, when I went to confession, I would promise not to do it again. But then again, sometimes I did. I would be better for a while, but then something would happen and I would lie again.

Some kids evade discovery of both their lies and their transgressions by becoming better at lying.

Don, the engineer, and a friend played a prank on a third boy and ably denied it. As he described this early adventure:

> I was about five or six, playing a game with another boy, and we saw another boy who we didn't care for very much who was playing by myself in a hole in the ground. He had taken his shoes off and left them outside the hole, so we decided to play a trick on him and we grabbed his shoes and we hid them.
>
> Well, soon he came out of the hole and he couldn't find his shoes, and so he went and told his mother. Then his mother told my mother that we had been playing nearby, and my mother asked me: "Did you take his shoes?" So I said: "No, of course not, in no way would we do this."
>
> So then we offered to help and we wandered around looking for his shoes, and finally we found them as if we had come across them by accident. And that was one of the times when my mother believed me. In fact, I remember her looking closely at me when I told her, as if she was looking for a sign that I wasn't telling the truth. But I could tell she couldn't tell whether I was or not. It felt a little scary at first, when I wasn't sure

whether she would believe me or not. But when she did, I
felt a little more confident that I could do this, that I was
able to trick my mother in this way.

Thus, while a lie might be caught, overall the people I spoke to
seemed to find they or others who lied were able to get away with it
or at least avoid any punishment if they were found out, thus perhaps
setting the stage for more lies. In fact, in some cases, their parents
might even overlook the lie or respond to its revelation by being
willing to help.

Lies to Conceal Unapproved Activities

Kids also learn to use lies to cover up unapproved activities. For
younger kids, common lies involve homework or other responsibilities. As kids get older, all sorts of lies sprout up around, as one
person I interviewed put it, "drugs, sex, and rock 'n' roll."

Stan, the high-school teacher, described some of the dubious
excuses he had become used to hearing from his kids.

I   They were supposed to be home by a certain time, but
    then they would be late, and they would say something
    like: "The teacher kept us after school." One time my
    daughter told me: "I had to go downtown with my friend.
    She wasn't feeling well." Another time my son said he
    stayed at school to watch the game. But there was no
    sick friend, there was no game. They just wanted to do
    something else.

These lies often worked, because even if exposed, Stan, like
other parents, might let them go or give a simple admonishment
because confronting the lie would be too much trouble, create too
much conflict. Dealing with such lies became a little like dealing
with brushfires—stamping them out if they became too serious,
looking the other way if they didn't, and knowing they would
probably start up again.

Teenagers start testing their independence and experiment with
all sorts of things that for parents are forbidden or taboo.

Alison, the counselor, had many such occasions to lie when she
was sixteen and wild about a boy. As she described it:

I   I had a boyfriend in another state when I lived in New
    York, and we had a very erotic, intimate relationship. I
    knew my parents wouldn't have understood, since I was
    only sixteen, so when I went to see him, I would

say that I was gong to stay with a girlfriend, but I made up this friend. Then, I would go to stay in his apartment for the weekend, and my parents never found out.

I did it because I have a very strong will, and when I really want something to happen, I'll make it happen no matter what.

In fact, I managed to see him one time when I was punished for something else. I was locked in my room, and my father said: "You cannot go out. You have to stay in your room." But I found a way to get out. Maybe I described some emergency that happened to my friend or something like that. I don't remember exactly. But I did get out and I got to see my friend.

Similarly, one of Stan's teenage daughters lied to conceal her drinking.

I   She was in high school, and one day she came home with her two front teeth chipped. When I asked what happened, she told me: "I slipped on the kitchen floor at my friend's house," and I knew that she had been there and there had been a party.

But the reason she slipped was because she had been drunk, although I didn't realize that at the time. Instead, she just said she had slipped while talking to someone in the kitchen, and all of her friends were backing her up. So I just believed her at the time.

And I similarly believed her when she said she was working on her studies, although I later realized she was doing a lot of fooling around with guys at school and cutting classes to do this. I just wanted to believe her, though later I realized there were many signs that this just wasn't true, such as her lack of success academically. But I just looked the other way for a long time, and eventually, as she got older, she did straighten up.

Other lies might be used to conceal illegal, immoral, deviant, or otherwise forbidden activities, such as using marijuana or other drugs, having sex, being gay, or dating someone from a different racial, ethnic, or religious group. However, lies also can be about something that's quite socially acceptable but they are told because the child just happens to have a different value system than his or her parents.

For example, Nancy, a business consultant, had this kind of experience when she was drawn toward going to church, although her family wasn't religious. As she told me:

I   When I was growing up, I lied about a lot of the standard things kids do just for survival.

And then there were other things I ended up lying about because there were things my parents didn't believe in, such as going to church. My parents weren't religious at all, and they had no idea that I decided I wanted to do this. But I felt I needed this in my life from the time I was a little kid, and so I would lie and tell them I was going somewhere else, when I was really going to church.

In fact, I had myself baptized when I was eight years old, but they never knew it.

Also, they had no idea that I spent a great deal of time with another family which really became like my real family to me. I just felt very alienated from my own family. So I retreated into a kind of fantasy world, and then I was drawn to this other family. But of course I felt I couldn't tell my parents I was drawn to this other kind of world, this other kind of life, so I just didn't. I kept it hidden and didn't tell them, so they never knew.

Because fear and uncertainty can lead to lies, some therapists encourage families to be more open and yielding in sharing their concerns.

Sexologist Dr. Louanne Cole commented:

I   I think that if families can talk more openly and candidly about anything, and not have taboo subjects that we don't talk about or taboo emotions that we don't dare to express, such as it's not okay to be angry, it's not okay to be sad, it's not okay to do this or that, then there can be less censorship and lying.

For example, parents or other adults may make the assumption that a young child shouldn't hear about sexual things.

And so when kids have questions about sex or these other things, they don't dare to ask mom and dad. So instead they try to ask a friend or find a magazine or they get some misinformation rather than ask their parents. Or if they try to bring up the subject, their parents may ask where they learned about that, and tell them, "Don't you dare talk about that subject again."

So that tells the kid never to bring up that subject again, and that shuts off communication or it leads to cover-ups and lies. If parents have a more candid attitude, that can lead to candor on the part of the child.

Lies to Impress

Children also may use lies to impress and build themselves up, or conceal their weaknesses—just like adults. For example, instead of talking about having large amounts of money or property to inflate their worth, kids talk about things like having a better toy, being more popular with playmates than they are, or having some special magical powers. But the basic impulse to show off and increase one's self-esteem seems the same.

Raphael, the healer, used lies to cover up his loneliness, anger, and feeling of abandonment when he was a child. But as he got older, he learned to bring such feelings out, and he felt better about being able to acknowledge the truth with others. It helped him feel closer to the people who were important in his life.

Lies may also be a way to cover up the little childhood thefts that children may resort to to impress or a way to get even or get revenge when they think someone has done something to hurt them.

Teenage Dating Lies

As kids become older, there are the familiar going-out and dating lies—focused around gaining more independence from parental and establishment rules.

The ID lies, for example, are probably quite famliar. To be able to drink or get into places when they are too young, kids try to pass for being older, and some even get a fake ID. Bartenders or doormen may be willing to go along with the pretense, as long as the person has the paperwork or appears old enough, because that means one more paying customer.

Typical dating lies are probably also quite familiar. They revolve around manipulating the dating game to get desired dates and get out of unwanted ones. For example, while males come up with come-ons to get dates or sex (i.e., "Of course, I love you" or "Everyone else is doing it"), females find ways to come up with believable excuses to gracefully turn someone down.

Stan, the high-school teacher, recalled a number of these:

I   I remember a couple of times using a lie to get out of a
     date. For example, there were times when I decided to
     cancel a date for some reason but I didn't want to say it,
     so it was easier to lie. Some examples might be that I just
     decided afterward that I didn't want to go out with the girl
     or something came up that I wanted to do more. But I
     didn't know how to say that nicely, so I would just make up
     an excuse.

     On the other hand, I knew there were many times
     that girls lied to me. For instance, some girl might say
     she couldn't go out with me because of some reason,
     but I would know it was a lie. It just didn't sound right or
     there would be something in her tone. But I figured, that
     was the way it was, and I didn't make a big deal about
     getting what I thought might be a phony excuse.

Sandy, the marketing consultant, recalled strategies she learned
from her mother and friends.

I always felt uncomfortable saying no when some boy
asked me out whom I didn't like. But of course you don't
tell someone "No, I don't want to see you because I don't
like you." So I learned very early to give excuses and even
be creative.

For example, I would say I was busy, already had
previous plans, had to baby-sit, or something like that.
And then if he became persistent, I would find other
reasons why I couldn't, such as I promised someone
else to do this or that.

But sometimes this kind of approach really did backfire,
because I remember once liking this boy who called me to
ask me out several times, when I really did have to baby-
sit. We had just had a fight and had broken up and he
wanted to get back together. Well, he asked me about
going out again on two different nights, and when I told
him about the baby-sitting, he just got mad. I tried to
explain it was really true and I did want to see him. But he
didn't believe me. And even though I called him back
saying I could cancel one of the evenings by telling the
people I was sick, it was too late. He was too hurt and
didn't want to go out with me anymore.

Lies to Help & Protect Others

Children learn early on to use lies to help and protect others, often with their parents showing them how and when to use such lies to conceal their feelings instead of coming out with the real, but hurtful or discomfiting truth.

Sandy learned the virtues of being less than forthright about things after she managed to thoroughly mortify her parents. As she described it:

I	I was about three or four at the time, and my parents had some of their friends and relatives over for a dinner. Well, while they were having dinner, I happened to wander up to the bathroom, and saw this little boy in there. Well, when I got back, I made this announcement that my daddy's thing was much bigger than little Jimmy's.

Well, needless to say, my parents and everybody else were really shocked, and afterward my parents talked to me to tell me there were things I shouldn't say even if they were true. It just wasn't polite to say such things, and then later I learned there were many other things I shouldn't say.

Parents may advise children on what they should say to cover up their real feelings or hide the truth to smooth over social relations, such as telling someone he or she looks good when the child doesn't think so or acting as if he likes the person when he does not. For example, I remember how my mother used to tell me things such as: "Now be nice to your cousin," or "Tell your aunt you liked her cake." It was part of what she called learning the social graces. Similarly, Blanche, the public-relations executive, covered up her real feelings about her sister, who was very much overweight.

I	I just learned early that it's good to protect people's feelings. For example, even though my sister was very fat, if she asked me: "Do I look pretty?" I would say: "Yes, you look beautiful to me," because I didn't want to tell her what I really thought. I wanted to make her feel better."

So, it's no wonder that people continue to lie in social situations and to protect and help others when they become adults. It's something they learned very early when they were children.

CHAPTER 11

Lying to Oneself

WHILE MOST LIES ARE DESIGNED TO DECEIVE OTHERS, people also lie to themselves—and for much the same reasons: to avoid some unpleasant truth or achieve some desired gain (or at least imagine one has achieved it).

For example, a man with a drinking problem may lie to himself that he has the problem. A woman with a personality flaw may pretend that she doesn't have this and find other more acceptable reasons for explaining why others don't have much contact with her. Someone with great dreams but little ability to realize them may fantasize that he can turn them into reality or imagine he already has. Such lies may turn into what appear to be lies to others, as the person acts on his own false beliefs and draws others into his reality (such as the travel promoter described earlier who came to believe in the fantasy of his travel programs). At the extreme end, such self-lies can turn into delusions, schizophrenias, and paranoias, which can lead to the mental hospital.

To some extent all of us lie to ourselves, if only to dream about possibilities. We enjoy the fantasy of getting away from everyday reality. Sometimes, if we act on these lies, we may be able to turn them into reality—such as in the Horatio Alger myth of a great desire that becomes true.

However, between these extremes are the bulk of the self-lies that are used for self-protection and gain as a kind of personal barrier against truth that might disrupt one's view of oneself or the world.

Why the Self-Lie?

Self-lies are self-protection, and they are, according to psychologist Daniel Coleman, who wrote a book about this subject, *Vital Lies, Simple Truths: The Psychology of Self-Deception,* a basic strategy used by the individual to protect against anxiety.' His main thesis is: The mind can protect itself against anxiety by dimming awareness; this mechanism creates a blind spot: a zone of blocked attention and self-deception; such blind spots occur at each major level of behavior from the psychological to the social.[2] In other words, we hide things from ourselves to keep ourselves from getting upset about something, which parallels some of our reasons for lying to others—to keep from upsetting our social relationships by smoothing them over with a lie.

According to Coleman, this use of self-deception through dimmer awareness has deep biological and psychological roots, and it operates much in the same way that the brain acts to relieve pain, such as by inducing numbness. As Coleman puts it:

> Whether physical or mental in origin, pain registers in the brain via a system that can dampen its signals. In the brain's design the relief of pain is built into its perception.

In particular, the brain uses a pain-numbing response in an emergency, which helps to induce calm. It's a life-saving strategy, Coleman points out, because once the individual is numbed and calm, he can better assess the situation.[4] While this kind of response developed early in evolution to help the individual survive physical dangers and pain, Coleman suggests this same kind of response occurs in reaction to psychological pain—such as an "affront to one's self-esteem, apprehension, or loss.'"

In turn, this denial and lying can take various forms. According to Goleman, citing a list of denial mechanisms described by psychiatrist Mardi Horowitz, we can deny in these various ways:

○ *Avoiding associations,* so we short-circuit the usual connections with something said or experienced because we don't want to experience them;

○ *Becoming numb,* so we turn off our emotions and don't feel the appropriate emotions;

○ *Showing a flattened emotional response,* so we constrict the usual expectable emotions we might feel;

○ *Dimming attention,* so we avoid focusing clearly on information, including thoughts, feelings, and physical sensations that might bring pain;

○ *Going into a daze,* so we cloud our alertness and avoid recognizing the significance of events we don't want to acknowledge;

○ *Constricting our thoughts,* so we don't explore the likely avenues of meaning beyond the obvious one;

○ *Experiencing memory failure,* so we are unable to recall events or their details, or we just selectively recall what happened again to blot out painful information;

○ *Disavowing what is so,* which involves saying or thinking that obvious meanings are not so, because we want to avoid them;

○ *Blocking through fantasy,* so we avoid reality or its implications by having fanciful thoughts of what might have been or could be.[6]

When we do deny, we aren't aware of it. Instead, the mind scans, filters, and selects information, and it does all this outside our conscious awareness.'

What information do we deny or deceive ourselves about? One big source is any information that threatens the self by not supporting how one feels about oneself, and therefore threatens self-esteem, according to Coleman, because such a threat is a major source of anxiety. The process is equivalent to the numbing reaction in animals. But whereas animals usually experience stress when their life is threatened, for humans, a challenge to their self-esteem is enough to trigger anxiety. And then that anxiety triggers the denial self-deception response.[8] For example, the mind starts selectively remembering events, or reinterpreting and slanting them.[9]

Lying about One's Own Abilities
or One's Business

One big source of self-lying concerns abilities, skills, and success in business, because ideas about accomplishment and achievement go to the heart of our self-esteem. If we do well, we feel good about ourselves. But if not, we feel bad, so there can be a great incentive to lie to oneself about personal failures.

Business-consultant Robert Middleton described how he noticed many of his clients had this problem. They at first didn't want to face the facts that their business wasn't doing well or that they were making key mistakes. But as things continued to spiral downward, they finally had to admit they needed help. As Middleton observed:

> A lot of people in business sometimes hold onto the belief that something has to be such and such a way. But it's not really true, and that can limit or destroy their business.
>
> For example, someone might think, I can only charge this amount. But who says so? Maybe he can really charge more. Or again, maybe someone thinks he should sell this, but the market isn't really there for it. So he just thinks he should try harder, when in fact, he should give that up and not try at all.
>
> Then, too, people can have self-limiting beliefs or beliefs that they can do more than they can. And either can hurt the business. On the one side, I think the self-limiting beliefs come out of fear. A person doesn't think that he can do all he can. But on the other hand, a person can build himself up so much that he ultimately falls. So there can be these two kinds of lies—lying about how great we really are or lying about how small we really are, and either can be damaging.

Besides leading to failure, other kinds of self-lies can make one miserable because one is doing more or something different than one wants. And they can lead to conflicts with others when one doesn't face up to what's really going on or what others need and want.

The Effects of Self-Lying in Relationships

Self-lying can also lead to problems in relationships because the reality of the relationship is out of step with what is wanted.

A good example of this is what happens in the codependency relationship, according to therapist Rose White, who specializes in codependency and addiction issues. In the codependency relationship, which is especially common in cases where one person is an alcoholic or addict, the partner—the codependent—modifies his or (usually) her life to adjust to the afflicted partner. But very often, this adjustment is based on living a lie or self-delusion, because the codependent is not seeing the truth about the partner or is denying his or her own needs or truths. As White commented:

> Codependency is a relationship in which we are not telling the truth about what our needs are. Usually, in the codependent relationship, there's a form of denial about what is going on presently, what has gone on in one's past, what has gone on in one's family life.
>
> Typically, the codependent is denying his needs and feelings. Emotional responses become flattened out, or reactions are projected onto something else, because the person is trying to deny or avoid recognizing what the actual situation is. He or she is trying to elude the truth. The person is lying to him or herself, though there's no awareness of this lying. It's not conscious and is used as a form of self-defense.

White gave examples of how such self-lying or denial could alter the course of the relationship.

> I have some clients that talk about how they have this wonderful, happy family, when that's not true at all. Or they say they have a terrific marriage when that's not true. They're just kidding themselves.
>
> But such lying is a form of protection, so they don't have to deal with what the true issues are, because many times, dealing with the true issues mean you have to do something about them.
>
> For instance, sometimes, if you face the facts, this might mean you have to leave your partner. Sometimes looking at the true issues may mean recognizing that you have denied yourself for your whole life for other people, and then you're left with this vacant, empty feeling, because you realize you have left yourself out.

Also, looking at the true issues might mean recognizing that you didn't have a happy childhood, that you had a miserable one, and you were never able to trust your parents because they never really protected you the way they were supposed to do.

Such recognitions can be very painful, and may mean the person has to do something about them to change them. And for many people that's hard, so they don't want to look.

Also, as White pointed out, people in codependency relationships might be deluding themselves about control issues and find it especially difficult to deal with them. She explained:

I   Codependency can range from being a good, helpful human being to being totally compelled to helping other people and controlling their life. And often, people lose sight of who's really in control.

For example, someone in a codependent relationship with an alcoholic may feel like she is keeping control, because she is the sober one. But in reality, what is happening is that she is being controlled by the other person's behavior.

So in dealing with codependents, a key aspect of therapy is helping the other person not only become aware of how he or she is deluding herself but in how to gain or regain control.

Other types of relationships may harbor self-delusion and denial, leading to anger and conflict. White described another couple she was seeing:

I   For eighteen years, everything has been seemingly wonderful. They've had what has seemed like a great marriage. But what has happened is that for eighteen years, she has gone along with everything that he has asked, according to her, and all of a sudden, she started realizing and admitting to herself that over all this time she has been denying herself things she's wanted.

What sorts of things? White continued:

0   Friends, relationships with other women, for example. The family unit was so important to them that she would do everything for the family.

For instance, her husband and son were involved in some male-dominated sport, and she went along with her husband and son in supporting them in this. But in reality she wasn't all that interested in this and felt left out, and her involvement in all their interests cut out her own.

So her husband, too, is upset and surprised, because he never knew what she really wanted, because she concealed it from him, since she was concealing it from herself. So now the healing involves bringing her real feelings out, discovering who she really is and wants, because she's concealed that part of herself from herself for so long.

Lying to Oneself about Personal Problems & Limitations

Self-delusion can be especially common when one has a personal problem or limitation one wants to avoid, especially a habit or addiction. Self-lies, such as "I don't have a habit," "I don't have an addiction," "I can stop whenever I want" can help protect the individual from accepting an uncomfortable truth.

Storm, the writer, experienced this with his own drinking problem. Eventually things got so bad and he got so much input from his friends, that he had to face the problem. As he described it:

My liquor problem got so far along that I couldn't deny it anymore. It was so obvious. I was turning yellow. I had trouble walking straight. I wasn't even drunk when this was happening. There was a continuous effect. Then, too, I was always sneaking a drink, and the pattern started to show to my friends.

It can be easy to be able to deceive one person. You can just slough off their complaints with some explanations or excuses. But when you try to do this with a lot of people, and they get together and talk about this, and they all tell you they know, then you know you've been nailed.

So eventually, I came to realize this and decided to go into a clinic to get over it. So that was for the best. But I felt bad that I had to get to that point, because I could have corrected the problem long before, if only I had the guts to face it when it first started happening. And then I also felt bad that I had been deceiving my friends into thinking everything was okay with me when it wasn't. At first, I guess I was successful, because I was lying to myself, too. And that makes it easier to lie to other people, when you actually end up believing it yourself, that you don't have a problem. But I did.

However, I finally came to recognize this, and I also came to realize that at a certain point you can't lie to yourself any more, because you're only fooling yourself. And eventually, if you do that long enough, you can destroy yourself, too. So at that point, I had to face what was true, and that's when I knew I had to change.

Overcoming the Self-Lie

One of the big problems with these self-lies is they can turn out to be even more devastating to the individual than the conscious lies to others, because they have the power to hurt the individual in two ways. First, he may hurt himself because he is not aware of his own lies and he may act on this false notion of what is true, with harmful results. Secondly, the individual who is acting or telling untruths that he is not aware of may end up having conflicts with others because of these lies. Plus, others may imagine he is untruthful as well.

How does a person overcome the lies to the self? Some of the therapists I spoke with emphasized the importance of making the individual aware of them. They pointed out that when a person was lying to himself or his therapist in treatment, the therapist could not help him in that area; it was necessary to first get to the truth and uncover and overcome the lie. But it could take a lot of personal work to do this because the person might be afraid of facing the truth.

Michael Gelbart, a therapist specializing in a combined mental and body approach to healing, observed:

I   Often, what a person says is just the tip of the iceberg to what is really going on in him or her, and he may not be aware of what this is. Thus, the person may not be consciously lying when I work with him and he hasn't told me some important thing about his life. In some cases, the person may just not think it's important and so doesn't say it. But in other cases, the person may be scared of saying what this is. Or the fear may be so deep that the person isn't even aware of how and what he really feels.

The only way I can help my clients is for them to tell me what is really going on for them. Often, even though a person may be sharing a lot, there's still a lot that is held back, because of all of the protections and fears, some of which are conscious, some of which are not. There are some things that clients may not be ready to reveal to me or themselves.

What sorts of things? Gelbart had a few suggestions:

Sometimes what is blocked are things the person is ashamed of, things that show him in a bad light, or maybe something he thinks is terrifying, hateful, or wrong about himself. Perhaps a person may be afraid of his or her own feelings in dealing with something if it comes to the surface, such as might be the case for someone who has been abused as a child. He or she might be afraid to say something for fear of not being believed, since many people aren't when they first reveal this. Or the person might fear that he'll be humiliated, shamed, or laughed at. For whatever reason he or she may hold this back.

At first this holding back may be conscious. But then it might also become repressed, so the person even denies this happened and the repression of something he doesn't want to face turns into the lie.

Rose White worked with clients with a codependency problem who were lying to themselves about their relationship. One of the first steps to help them was to get them to be aware of what they were doing, including the double messages they were sending themselves, so they could overcome them. As she commented:

D All of us have been trained to give double messages to some extent. We were trained to not tell the truth in certain circumstances, to tell little white lies, to be nice even when we didn't feel nice, to smile when we didn't feel like smiling.

Well, when you are consciously doing that and in control of the process, that's one story. That can be healthy because then the person is coming from a place of choice. He or she knows what he or she is doing. But when a person continually denies his real feelings and thoughts, there's a problem.

Thus, one key to a successful therapy is to help make the person conscious of what's real for him so he can be responsible for his own life. He can make the choices he wants, because he is aware of what those choices are.

To get to this point might be quite difficult because of the individual's resistance to looking at the problem. Much of therapy might involve helping to support the person in looking at this painful past so he or she can face it and move on. For example, say the person has created self-delusions to cover up fears and inadequacies dating from childhood. A therapist might work with the person this way, according to White:

> Say the person is lying to himself as a form of protection to keep his sanity, say because he was neglected or abused in his childhood or because his parents simply weren't there for him.
>
> In the therapeutic process, what may happen is some of these truths may start emerging. Now, as things start opening up and revealing themselves, it may feel like a horror story. Because the process is like opening Pandora's box in some way. Well, that's when people truly need to have a support system around them, and that's when it's very helpful working with a therapist or perhaps a support group.
>
> Then, too, it can be useful to have this outside support, because as a person goes through recovery in a codependent situation, the other partner may do everything he or she can to subvert this change, even though they may not be aware of what they are doing. It's like the wife who decides to go on a diet, and the husband brings her a box of chocolates to subvert her efforts, to keep her the way she has always been. So the person gets a double message.
>
> Thus, in any therapy, it's important to look at the whole family system any person is involved in as well as the way they may have been deluding themselves, because the family is a system, and any system maintains itself by seeking a form of homeostasis or balancing itself out.

As a result, if one person changes in a family, the family will do what it can to pull that person back, to keep them the way they have been before. Thus, it's necessary to let the client know that people may not like them changing, may not like them giving up their past self-lies, because this change is going to make the other people uncomfortable. So they have to work on working out these adjustments with others as they let go of their lies. And all this can be a difficult process—not only facing the truth, but also maneuvering through this process of change that the truth brings in its wake.

CHAPTER 12

The Strategy of Deceiving & Perceiving

W hy is lying so common? Are people who lie simply good at deceiving? Or are people who are lied to poor at perceiving? And what can be done to deal with lying? How can people recognize when someone is lying? How do people learn how and when to use a lie when it might seem justified, such as to keep someone from knowing information that may be harmful to him?

The Success of Deception

Lying is common because, in general, the ability to deceive is better than the ability to perceive. In other words, lying works because people more often will be able to get away with it than people will be able to recognize the lie.

This development is linked to the evolution of lying as a survival and defense mechanism discussed earlier. To briefly recap here, researchers have found that the ability to deceive can help an organism survive, so the genetic capability for deception has evolved through natural selection. As psychologist Charles Bond and others point out, for hundreds of generations, those who are the most cunning have left more offspring, while those who are less cunning have left fewer, so the ability to deceive has increased in the gene pool.'

When Bond and his colleagues set up a research study in which undergraduates told lies and truths about their own job, the liars were able to conceal their lies from most observers, with only about a quarter of the lies being detected.[2] Other psychological experiments on lying and detection have had similar results. For instance, when R. E. Kraut reviewed the results of nine studies judging whether people told the truth, he found that, on the average, the participants were able to make accurate judgments only about half of the time.[3] In turn, applying a correction for chance guessing, Bond and his colleagues estimated that only about 14 percent of the would-be detectors were able to expose the typical liar in a psychological experiment.[4]

The greater success of deceivers is also shown by the problems of people who are trained in lie detection. For example, when Kraut and D. Poe studied a group of U.S. customs inspectors—lie detectors by profession—they found the inspectors couldn't reliably expose deceit,[5] a finding that may be expected, considering the obvious failure of inspectors to stop more than a small percentage of the people who smuggle various goods and drugs through customs.

According to researchers, this better ability to deceive than perceive lies makes survival sense. Bond says:

> ı Though both deception and lie-detection capabilities have been naturally selected, they may not have evolved to comparable levels. Deception skills may have evolved further. If so, one may infer that—over generations—an organism's survival has depended more on its ability to deceive than its ability to detect deceit . . (For example) the rabbit runs faster than the fox, because the rabbit is running for his life, while the fox is only running for his dinner. This "life-dinner" principle of unequal selection pressure could explain the imbalance in the deceptive struggle.[6]

There are a number of reasons why perceiving lies may be so difficult. Not only may perceivers be unable to tell when skillful

liars are lying, they may think that truth-tellers who seem deceptive are lying, too. This is what researchers call the Othello effect.
In Shakespeare's classic, Othello, the character falsely accuses
Desdemona of infidelity, believing her emotional outburst at this
accusation to be further proof of her lies. In fact, he is mistakenly
interpreting her fear of being disbelieved. When Charles Bond
and associate William Fahey investigated this difficulty of sorting
truth from lies, they found this quite true. Subjects seeing video-
tapes of people lying or not lying about their feelings could not
distinguish the lies from the truth.'

Research on sales pitches has shown that experienced sellers
may be so good in their ability to deceive that they fool subjects who
are cued to look for the body movements and speech patterns
associated with deception. The problem is that although the judges
might pick up nonverbal cues associated with lying, these cues
don't correlate with the seller's lie. Thus the researchers in these
studies have concluded that experienced sellers, confident in their
ability to deceive and having no qualms about doing so, are not
likely to inadvertently give away their lies with nonverbal cues.[8]

Why can't people perceive lies? Generally, the people I spoke
to talked about being unaware or gullible. They didn't pay attention or didn't know the cues of lying, or they just tended to
believe _ or wanted to believe—that someone was telling the truth.
As a result, the usual discovery of a lie tended to occur when
something the liar said just didn't seem to make sense or fit
something the listener knew from before—or later on, when the
inconsistencies contained in the lie began to unravel.

For Don, the engineer, the big cue to a lie came through
external information that showed up the lie, but otherwise it
was hard to tell. As he commented:

II   It's hard to know if someone is lying, unless you have
       some sort of validity check that comes up. Otherwise
       you don't know. For example, suppose somebody says
       X, and the result is Y, then that's an indicator that there
       was something wrong. Otherwise there may be no way
       to tell if someone's lying.
           Or another possibility might be if something doesn't fit
       someone's usual pattern—such as say someone says
       he just likes to go to thrilling movies, but then he wants to
       see a calm, thoughtful one, you might wonder about the
       discrepancy. There's a lack of congruity that might

suggest a lie. But otherwise, who knows? It's usually
hard to pick up anything in someone's voice or tone.

The Strategies for Telling a Lie

What makes a successful liar so good? What strategies do liars use?

Good liars, according to psychologists Bella DePaulo, Julie
Stone, and Daniel Lassiter, are aware of the attitudes and preferences of the targets of their lies.' They may even construct their
lies with such information in mind, much like the salesman who
figures out what to say to push the prospect's button, or the so-
called "psychic" or "spiritual reader" who senses what her customer wants to hear and then says it.

Secondly, good liars learn to control "channels" to present
themselves in a convincing way. Generally, the verbal channel is
most easily managed, and it's also the channel that's especially
important for listeners as they hear words, react to them, and
hold the speaker accountable for what he says. They also may be
able to control the nonverbal channels of communication, such
as their face, body, and tone of voice, although researchers such
as DePaulo, Paul Ekman, and others have found that these
channels are much more difficult to control, because emotional
reactions are registered automatically.[10]

On the other hand, as liars become more motivated to lie
successfully, they may actually lose some of their advantage because
they may pay too much attention to what they are saying and not
enough to the nonverbal cues they are giving off. This is what
DePaulo and her associates found in an experiment with male and
female college students who sent and received **truthful** and deceptive
messages. The more the subjects were motivated to lie, because they
found their targets more attractive, the more their lies were
detected. This led the researchers to conclude that the senders paid
more attention to the more salient verbal channel they felt they
could control more (i.e., what they were saying) and less to the
nonverbal cues, which were what eventually gave them away."

The Strategies for Perceiving a Lie

Although it may be difficult to distinguish the truth from a lie,
there are techniques that help even up the odds, though they may
not be correct all the time. These techniques don't always work
because it is easy to err in either direction—misinterpreting seemingly suspicious behavior for a lie when the person is telling the

truth, which is called the Othello effect; or not noticing little behavior cues or verbal inconsistencies that point to a lie.

Researchers have found certain patterns of behavior that may point to a lie. Many have been discovered by a San Francisco psychologist, Paul Ekman, who has studied techniques used by liars.

According to Ekman, there are two types of clues to deceit. These clues essentially are mistakes that reveal the truth or may suggest that what was said or shown is untrue without revealing the truth. One clue is "leakage," which occurs when the liar's behavior suggests he or she is lying without revealing the truth.[12] Then, too, there may be something in the overall social context in which the lie occurs that gives off clues that things aren't quite right.

Discovering Leakages

Leakages may be the most difficult to discover, because these usually come from verbal slips, and the liar usually has control over the verbal channel. But the liar may not always remember what he says or to whom. So there may be inconsistencies and contradictions that build up. Later on, the liar may give the wrong name or information to someone, so he must backtrack to conceal the holes. Such discrepancies can be a clue to lying, but not always, because people really do forget and make mistakes.

Still another reason, pointed out by Ekman, is that liars can't always anticipate when they will need to lie. So they don't always have the time to prepare the line to be taken, to rehearse and memorize it.[13] Even if the liar has had plenty of advance notice and has prepared what he is going to say, he may not be able to anticipate all the questions or think through his answers, so he may slip up, be unconvincing, or even blurt out the truth.[14] Or the liar may forget what he has said previously and have trouble answering new questions quickly and confidently. In short, as Ekman sums up, any of these three common types of failures can produce easily spotted clues to deceit!'

Discovering Deception Clues

Assuming the liar maintains control over the verbal channel or his little inconsistencies or slips are unnoticed or overlooked, the other big key to perceiving lies comes through the behavioral or "deception" clues the liar gives away.

In this case, there are a number of major types of clues, again suggested by Ekman's research. These include the way a line is spoken, the difficulties a person may have in lying about his feelings (including his feelings about lying, his fear of being caught, his guilt at deceiving another, and his delight at making someone else a dupe). As Ekman points out, these signs of guilt, fear, or delight can show up in the person's facial expression, voice, or body movement, even when the liar is trying to conceal them. Even if there is no nonverbal leakage, the struggle to prevent these leaks may produce a deception clue.[16]

Here are key clues that can be a sign of lying (though sometimes not—remember the Othello effect).

O *Carefully considering each word before it is spoken.* This can occur because the liar hasn't thought through what to say next to keep the pretense going or has trouble remembering what was said. So he may need to be more careful in thinking about what to say. Thus, pauses during speech or other gestures associated with thinking might be a clue.

O *The difficulty in concealing or falsely portraying emotions.* Real emotions may leak out, or, if the person is trying to feign an emotion, it may be hard to do this, too. According to Ekman, there are two big problems in concealing emotions. The first is that when an emotion begins gradually or is only slightly felt, the changes in behavior are small and could be readily concealed if the person was aware of them. But many people may not be aware of such changes, and so don't control them. On the other hand, if the emotion should be a strong one, then the problem is in controlling it, and it can be difficult to conceal the changes in the person's face, body, or tone of voice. Even if the person can conceal these changes so his real feelings don't leak out, the struggle itself can be noticeable and so provide a clue. Falsifying emotions can be problematic, too, because the deceiver must put together the right movements and changes of the voice that reflect a particular emotion, and many people may find it quite difficult to perform these movements voluntarily.[17]

O *The way the person feels about lying.* The emotions associated with the fear of being caught, one's guilt about lying, or one's delight in duping another person might be the giveaway. Signs of nervousness and anxiety could be a clue that one is fearful of being trapped in a lie, although the danger here is the Othello effect, since, as Ekman notes, "it is always a problem to distinguish between the innocent's fear of being disbelieved and the guilty person's detection apprehension." This problem is even worse when the perceiver is known to be suspicious or has caught the liar in a lie before. Conversely, as the liar becomes more practiced and has more success, this fear of being caught will go down, although the risk to the liar of making careless errors grows. So, according to Ekman, some degree of detection apprehension helps the liar by keeping him more alert. But too much apprehension can give him away, because of the difficulty in controlling these emotional clues." Moreover, as the stakes get higher this apprehension can increase because, initially, the person tells a lie to gain a reward or advantage. After a while, the rewards may no longer be available, but the person has to maintain the deceit to avoid getting caught and being punished for the lie.[20]

Also, a person may experience guilt just because of lying and that can be a clue as well. This guilt may turn out to be more than the person anticipated, or it can increase over time if the liar finds that his original lie was not enough, and now he has to repeat it or must even elaborate and expand upon it to protect the original lie.[21] Ekman also points out circumstances when such guilt can be most severe and hence most likely to give away the liar, such as when the person's lies are not authorized by some higher or legitimate authority or when the person lied to is trusting and doesn't gain or suffers from the lie as much or more as the liar.[22]

Finally, there may be some people who let their delight at duping the victim give them away.[23] They brag about their lie to others, who reveal them or show signs of excitement or enjoyment at lying, which betrays the lie.

O *The behavioral cues from the liar's words, voice, or body.* According to Ekman, liars usually give off behavioral cues, because they are not able to monitor, control, and disguise all of their behavior. As a result, liars usually concentrate on concealing or falsifying what they expect others to watch most, which is usually their choice of words and then their facial expression. Liars control their words because they know they will be held more accountable for what they say. And, they are likely to try to control their face, because it receives the most attention from others.[24] Even then there can be leaks and clues from the voice or face.

These facial and voice cues can be especially important giveaways because the individual's face and voice are directly connected to those areas of the brain involved with emotion, whereas the person's words are not, according to Ekman. When a person's emotions are aroused, the muscles on his face begin to fire invol-

untarily, and there will be changes in his voice. Although a person
can learn to interfere with and override these involuntary reactions,
there can still be leaks, such as when a person forgets to exercise
this conscious control or when he initially experiences the
emotional arousal, before applying the conscious brakes.[25]

The body is more subject to conscious control, because most
body movements are not directly tied to the areas of the brain
involved in emotion, as Ekman notes. But most people don't
bother to control their body cues, because they have grown up
thinking such controls are not necessary, since people are usually
not held accountable for what they reveal through the actions of
their body. Rather, the emphasis is on watching the face or evaluating the words to detect lies, so people just ignore the body.[26]

Then, too, there might be a discrepancy between what the
person says and what his voice, body, or face reveals, which can
point to a lie.[27]

In his book, *Telling Lies,* Ekman describes a number of the major
clues in the words, voice, or body that suggest lies. Some of the key
clues:

0 Words. Liars might be given away by such things as slips of the
tongue, forgetting familiar names, and mistakes in reading or
writing.[28] Sometimes the build-up of emotion, concealed by the lie,
might escape through an emotional outburst or tirade, which can
lead to specific slips of information, too.[29] Also, evasions or
circumlocutions may be giveaways although some liars are too
smart to be evasive and indirect. Sometimes a person is normally
evasive and indirect in the way he speaks, so this isn't always a
signal of lying.[30]

O The voice. A big clue to deceit is too long or too frequent pauses.
This is a sign the person is trying to think about or craft a
response. Another may be speech errors, including non-words
such as "ahs" and "uhhs," and repetitions or partial words. The
sound of the voice, particularly pitch, can signal an emotion underlying the lie, such as the person's fear, anger, or other feelings of
upset. Ekman notes that pitch becomes higher when someone is
upset or excited, while the pitch may drop when the person feels
sadness or sorrow. Making it even worse for the liar is the fact that
changes in the voice due to emotion are not easy to conceal,
especially if the lie is designed to cover up emotions felt at the
moment or if the lie itself has led the person to feel a strong
emotion." On the other hand, the voice isn't always a giveaway,
because some people may not show emotion in their voice, or a

person may not be emotional about a particular lie. So someone's voice can be calm even though he is lying.[32]

0 *The body.* Some of the key clues to lying come through what Ekman calls "emblems" and "illustrators." Emblems are specific gestures with a particular meaning to a particular cultural group, such as a wave that means hello or good-bye or a head nod for yes. However, when there is a slip in the way an emblem is normally performed or only a small part of the emblem is performed, this could be an indication that the person has something to conceal.[33] An example of this might be the person who starts to raise his middle finger in a traditional gesture of anger, but then thinks the better of it and instead responds with a smile suggesting friendliness. Likewise, an unconsciously performed gesture outside of the normal position in which it is used could be a clue.

Illustrators are the open movements that illustrate speech, such as a big, open gesture to describe a large house. In this case, according to Ekman, the clue to deceit is not in the particular illustrator used, since these can vary with personality style or culture, but in the decrease in the number of illustrators normally used by a person. The reason for this is that people tend to use more illustrators when they are very involved in what is being said, because then they are more excited or aroused in some way, whether positively or negatively. But when people use fewer illustrators than usual, it could be because they are being cautious about what they are saying, which sometimes may be due to deceit. If people are trying to feign an emotion, they may be given away by their failure to illustrate as much as they would usually do if their heightened emotional arousal were true." However, to interpret these clues correctly it is necessary to know what the person usually does. If you meet someone for the first time, you generally can't use illustrators, though sometimes an emblematic slip might give a person away.

The other major type of body movement is what Ekman refers to as "manipulation." Essentially this occurs when one part of the body (often the hand or a finger) manipulates another body part (such as by massaging, rubbing, scratching, pinching, and the like). Many people think an increase in such movements is a sign of deceit because when people are uncomfortable or nervous they fidget or make restless movements. But Ekman considers such movements quite unreliable. One reason is that many people show an increase in these movements when they are relaxed and feel they can let their hair down, so they let go of their formal controls. Then, too, people vary a great deal in the types of manipulators they use and how often, so a prior knowledge of the person is generally necessary to evaluate him. Also, people may use more manipulators when they are uncomfortable about anything, not just lying. Finally, it's relatively easy to inhibit these manipulators, so a person who is lying can often succeed in controlling them.[35]

O *The autonomic nervous system.* Ekman also suggests that changes produced by the autonomic nervous system due to emotional arousal could be another source of clues to deception. These are the sorts of changes measured by the lie detector. Many of these changes are visible, such as changes in the pattern of breathing, frequency of swallowing, amount of sweating, and the changes reflected in the face, such as blushing, blanching, and the dilation of the pupils:[38] According to Ekman, the autonomic-nervous-system changes appear to be specific for each emotion, so that an aware person might be able to tell just by observing not only whether a person is emotionally aroused, but what emotion he really feels. Moreover, such observations might be especially telling because these reactions are relatively difficult to censor, whereas other body and facial reactions may be more readily controllable.[37]

O *The face.* Still other signals of lying can come from the face, again because real emotions trigger facial responses involuntarily, although a person can control and interfere with these actions, according to Ekman.[38] What is especially helpful in deciphering real feelings is the fact that some facial expressions, such as those indicating happiness, fear, anger, disgust, sadness, and distress, are universal, and many others may be, too.[39] As a result, while people can sometimes be taken in by false expressions (such as the friendly smile of an enemy), many times people can see the real feelings leak out through a person's facial features. According to Ekman, people may be fooled because when people lie, "their most evident, easy-to-see expressions, which people pay most attention to, are often the false ones." By contrast, people usually miss the more subtle signs and fleeting hints that reveal the true and concealed emotions.[40] Some of these are what Ekman refers to as "microexpressions," which flash on and off the face in less than a quarter of a second, and these are an indicator of the emotion that is really felt.[41] However, these don't occur very often. Instead, what is more common and telling, Ekman has found in his research, are the "squelched expressions," which are the emotional responses that are suppressed just as they are beginning and the liar becomes aware of them. Since the liar doesn't want this response to show, he shuts it off, sometimes covering it up with another expression, such as a smile, which is the most common cover or mask.[42]

While there is always the chance of being wrong—because some liars are experts at controlling their features, while others may just be showing emotion because they are upset, not because they are lying—there are clues to lying from these subtle sources of expression. Some of the major ones reported by Ekman are these:

0 Increased blinking or pupil dilation are signs of increased emotional arousal and could indicate lying if this is the source of the arousal and not some other emotion such as the fear of being disbelieved.[43]

0 Blushing, which is a signal of shame or guilt, could suggest the liar is embarrassed or ashamed about what he is concealing. Or the person could simply be embarrassed. Also, the face reddened with anger could be a sign of hidden anger underlying a lie.'"

O Blanching, a response to controlled anger or fear, may be a sign of a concealed emotion, too, though so far not much is known about this response.[45]

O Increased eyeblinks, pupil dilation, or facial sweating, as signals of increased emotional arousal, may also be clues that something is going on, although these can be triggered by various emotions, too.[46]

In addition, the face may betray a person's attempt to feign an emotion, such as when a person tries to show he really cares for someone but doesn't or a salesperson tries to fake his enthusiasm. Some of the cues to look for include:

O Any facial expression that lingers for five seconds or more, such as a prolonged smile or look of amazement because most real facial expressions fade after four or five seconds.[47]

O Crooked or asymmetrical facial expressions, such as a crooked smile. Most people cannot control all movements of their facial muscles, so when they try to fake something, they can't get the expression exactly right.[48]

O Smiles that show a muscular action around the lips, such as a narrowing or tightening, can indicate a hidden negative emotion such as anger, disgust, fear, contempt, or sadness. By contrast, true smiles don't show this muscular movement, and instead show a movement of the outer muscle that circles the eye.49

O Facial expressions that are out of synch with body movements or with the usual location in the flow of speech or changes in the voice. These suggest the person is trying to control and falsify an emotion. For example, anger is likely to be expressed before or at the beginning of a statement (i.e., "I don't like what you are doing"). But if the facial expression comes afterward, it is more likely that the person might be just trying to act as if he were angry.[50]

Ekman identifies dozens of smiles associated with different emotions, including fear, contempt, and misery. By knowing the differences, the perceiver may be able to pick up when a person is trying to manufacture an outward appearance and when he is expressing what he really thinks.

In short, there may be numerous clues to lying in what a person says, how he says it, and in the emotional reactions he expresses in his voice, face, and various parts of his body. If a perceiver pays close attention and is knowledgeable about these clues, he may be more able to pick up lies. At best, being aware of these clues can only increase the possibility of identifying the liar, since these clues can also arise because the person is feeling other emotions. Then, too, some people are good at controlling emotional expressions or masking them.

Discovering Clues in the Overall Social Context

There may also be clues in the social setting itself, notably in interactions that indicate something is being hidden or in special arrangements made to conceal or hold back the flow of information (such as a seemingly greater-than-usual effort to look something up). For example, author and management-consultant Judith Briles described clues that might be found in a business setting:

|| Say people are talking about you or saying something they don't want you to hear. You can usually tell this when you walk into a room and silence falls.

Or suppose an employer walks into a room, and all of a sudden things get shuffled together or books get closed. That can indicate things that the employees don't want the employer to see.

Another sign that things may be hidden in the workplace are phone calls that are very hush-hush. Or maybe there's an unexpected abruptness. Also, a lot of things may get locked up all the time, or there may be many meetings behind locked doors.

Still another clue may be when an employee asks a question he feels is legitimate to understand something that he perceives going on in the office, but he doesn't get a straightforward answer. This may suggest that something unusual is up.

Clues to Look For

There may be clues that experts in lie detection such as Ekman look for, but I also wondered about the clues that common people usually look for.

In general, the people I spoke with indicated they could easily be duped and often were unaware of people lying to them. Yet, there were indicators that led them to be suspicious.

For example, inconsistencies or claims that didn't make sense were one sign. Also, there were certain types of statements that raised red flags that someone might be lying, such as someone bragging about social-status symbols, suggesting they weren't all that they said they were and were compensating to make up for it.

People also may see nervousness as a sign of lying. Dick, the sales executive, looked for such clues in customers. As he commented:

I   I find it difficult for a customer to lie because he knows he's lying. What do I look for? I find customers have a hard time looking you in the eye. They also fidget. They're interrupted frequently and welcome interruptions. Also, they try to get the meeting over fast, because it's not comfortable for them. The situation is tense, they're tense. It's just not normal.

Other signs were the clash between body language and the message the person was saying. Raphael, the healer, tended to be quite conscious of this when he worked with clients.

0   I look for an incongruence in the way they are and what they're saying. if things are just not jibing, that leads me to suspect that someone might be lying. What kind of incongruence? Well, there may be a discrepancy between the tone of the voice and what they're telling me they really feel about something. So I listen for that, or

sometimes, just get a gut feeling I can't really explain—
something just doesn't feel right.

Alternatively, a person pushing something too hard might be a
danger sign, too, especially in a sales or persuasion type of situation.
As Reba, the speaker, observed:

> When someone's coming on so strong, it just makes
> me wonder if they're sincere. Why are they pushing so
> hard? I think that if they were really being honest, would
> they have to sell that hard? So that kind of behavior
> leads me to distrust.

Much of the time, people felt they were at the mercy of practiced
liars. Storm, the writer, described this frustration:

0   Sometimes you just can't know. Say someone is really
    lying. Well, usually, they'll be poker-faced. They won't
    give any clues away. And then people are so different;
    there's a different read on everybody, and some are
    able to lie better than others, or people lie in different
    ways.
        And usually there's no one tip-off cue, like suddenly
    the person starts looking out of the window or doesn't
    meet your eye. In my experience, the people who are
    good at lying do meet you in the eye because they are
    used to being bald-faced liars. So eye contact doesn't
    give me any clues.
        For me, the best thing is to know what we're talking
    about, so I can call the person on something if it doesn't
    seem right. And then maybe they'll get nervous and
    fidgety because I seem to be onto them. But others
    may just plow ahead with some logical explanation as if
    nothing is wrong.

That seems to be the way it is for most people. They pick up on
occasional clues such as inconsistent information, incongruent
behavior, or signs of evasiveness and nervousness, but still very
often are duped or just don't know.

Perhaps if people learned to pay more attention to the clues to
lying they might be better at knowing when someone is lying. But,
as the experts have pointed out, as the perceivers get better, so do the
liars in this never-ending escalation of the ability to lie versus the
ability to perceive.

Conclusion

*A*s THE PRECEDING CHAPTERS HAVE ILLUSTRATED, we may say we don't like to lie, but often we do. It is a way to defend ourselves or gain rewards. Then we usually find justification as to why we do it, and at the same time decry we the lies of others.

Lies strike us as hurtful, as betrayals, as indicators of uncertainty, because they make us unsure about relationships, about whether promised things will happen, about whom and what we can trust.

In turn, there is a biological basis for lying—for the ability to lie, to be good at it, to get away with it has been programmed into us from our animal heritage. Deceit is a survival mechanism, and those with the greater ability to be deceitful survive. The paradox here is that those with the greater ability to detect deception have been more apt to survive as well. Overall, the probabilities favor the likelihood that people will lie. Perhaps using a kind of conscious or unconscious cost-benefits analysis, they weigh the risks of telling the lie against the importance and degree of the potential gains or defensive advantages in telling that lie. And maybe they factor in the guidelines of traditional morality and current social practice in deciding when and what lies to tell.

Here comes another paradox. Traditional morality forbids lies. The principle is encoded in the religious teachings and in the folk tales and stories that we hear as a child, such as in the ancient *Pinocchio* story. Yet so often our social activities demand a lie, such as the white lie designed to help smooth over social relationships or keep someone unknowing about something harmful.

There is continuous tension between the immediate gains to the liar versus the potential damages to society if the lie is told or the truth is concealed. It's as if lying helps to illuminate what has always been a source of tension in human society—the desire to act out of the self-interest of the individual versus the need to conform to the demands of the social order. Most individuals usually use the lie for personal ends, while social groups discourage the lie because of its power to disrupt relations. Yet at times the truth can be more disruptive or damaging, such as when knowing that truth disrupts a personal relationship or makes a society vulnerable.

To Confront or Not to Confront the Lie?

Suppose you suspect or know of a lie or a concealment. Do you confront it?

The answer is: It depends—it depends on your personal style, on the nature of the relationship, on the importance of the situation, on the potential gains versus the losses of exposure, and so on.

A common response for much of everyday, not very important social lying is to simply let the lie go to avoid hurting people's feelings, embarrassing them, or disrupting relationships with a confrontation over something relatively trivial. Letting it go may be a good strategy for many minor lies if we don't want to derail an otherwise good social or business relationship.

Is the Confrontation Worth It?

Deciding whether to confront the lie sometimes results in an analysis in which the victim will bring it up if he sees a payoff for doing it. But if there's no gain, he lets it go.

Others considered confrontation in terms of the importance or endurance of the relationship. If it is just a casual social encounter, they might let the lie go, feeling the relationship too fleeting to merit raising the issue. But if the relationship is an ongoing or long-term one, they might say something to deal with the lie, because it would interfere with closeness and trust.

Robert Young, the therapist I spoke with, had this advice:

| My advice on what to do would depend on their relationship to that person who has lied to them in the first place. If it's a spouse or a family member or someone they are close to, I think people tend to confront it and should, because they're going to have to continue to be in a relationship with that person, whether they raise the issue or not. I think with a boss or co-worker, it's the same sort of situation. It can be difficult to live or work together if one person suspects a lie.

However, if the lie is from someone one has met in passing, then I would suggest that the best strategy might be to simply avoid them because they aren't trustworthy. But there may be no reason to confront them, because there's no need for a continuing relationship. It's just as easy to avoid them and deal with the lie that way.

The Importance of Being Diplomatic or Tactful

Suppose someone does decide to confront. How should he do it? A good approach is to be tactful and diplomatic so the person who has lied has a way out, can save face, or feels support for confessing. Then the liar is most likely to reveal the truth and not get angry and defensive about doing so.

On the other hand, if a person is too openly confronted, he might react as if he were being attacked or invaded, making him angry and increasing the possibility of conflict—and perhaps more lies to cover up.

Raphael, the healer, described the dangers of confronting someone too openly:

I once lost a client because I found I was too confrontational in trying to get him to face the truth. I thought our relationship could withstand it, and it didn't.

So I think it's very important to take into consideration the timing and be sensitive about how someone is going to receive something. That way he may be more ready to face the truth.

On the other hand, if the lie is important enough, if the relationship is important enough, and if confrontation fits with one's personal style, then it might be good to confront. In fact, some of the therapists I spoke to generally recommended this as beneficial both for the individual and the relationship.

Therapist Sylvia Mills emphasized the need to check out and confront inconsistencies, such as one might check out something in a house that didn't seem quite right. As she put it:

> I think if people feel or suspect they are in a situation where someone is lying about something that matters, they should check it out, the same way they would check out the wood and the floorboards when buying a house. How? You go and you stamp on the floor in a few places, put some pressure on it, and test it. Likewise, I think people should test out things in a relationship when they have suspicions. If you have an "instinct" something is not right, apply a little pressure to see if the person is feeling and thinking inside the way he is presenting himself on the outside. You need to do this for your own psychological health and the good of the relationship.

Then, too, confronting the lie might lead to a sense of release, leading to feelings of greater personal strength, a closer relationship, or the removal of barriers to a business or personal relationship.

For example, Sara, the educator, felt renewed strength when she began confronting the man she was in a relationship with about things he had lied about or concealed. As she described it:

> At one time, I thought it better to save face or not confront people. But I came to realize that this was because I wasn't willing to be in my own power and say what was really happening. And that was because I was insecure myself. I was afraid of rejection, afraid that I wasn't going to be accepted. I was afraid to make someone else angry or upset by bringing up something I knew to be the truth. But what I didn't realize at the time was that I was losing my own self-respect and their respect by not calling them on it when they weren't being honest with me or by saying what I really felt about something.
>
> For example, a man I was in a relationship with was relating something that happened to us, which wasn't so, and at one time I would have just let this go.

But this time I called him on it, and I reminded him about what really happened, and he finally admitted what really did. So I was willing to say that something was a lie, which was new for me. And I felt much better about myself when I did.

Giving hints that one might know something and giving the person a chance to retreat and change his story or explain might also be an effective strategy in some cases.

For example, Dick, the sales executive, described how he used this approach effectively with his clients:

I   When I sense someone is lying or fudging, I don't believe in calling them on it directly. I think that's cutting off your nose to spite your face, because that just makes people defensive or hostile. They feel challenged and that can put them on guard.

What I do is I let them know in a subtle way that I question what they are saying, and I would just like to see some support for this. And I also might allow that I could be wrong or not understand them exactly. So I give them a chance to back down.

For instance, say we're talking about price, and they give me a quote that seems out of line. I might say something like: "Well, we'll be glad to match that pricing as soon as you can show me in writing the competitor's quote," and then I'll move onto a different area to give the person a feeling of space. Then, if he does show me some supporting evidence to back up what he has said, I'll go along with his proposal. But if not, there's just a tacit understanding he'll accept my view of things and my proposed rate. So his attempt to state something that's wrong just isn't brought up again. That way I'm not directly challenging him on it; I'm not trying to suggest he's a liar. So he can back down quietly if my suspicions are correct, and at the same time the business relationship can go on.

Similarly, Blanche, the public-relations executive, used much the same approach when she had suspicions about her employees. As she put it:

I   Say I suspect someone in the office of doing something, like taking things, but I don't have any proof. I

think it's important to use tact. For instance, in a meeting I might let them know that I've noticed that things
are missing, that things have been disappearing, and I
might ask if they have noticed any of their things disappearing, too.

Likewise, if I've said something that's not true, say at
a staff or client meeting, I would feel better if someone
just gently said: "Well, Blanche, that's not exactly the
way it is; it's this way," rather than trying to catch me in
an exaggeration or lie. Then, I might simply say: "Oh,
there I go again," and let it drop. I'll feel I've got a way
out, a way to save face, because I may know they know
I've tried to bend the truth a little, but they haven't made
a big deal about it, either, so I can more easily back out.

Providing a supportive environment for helping the person
reveal the truth can work well, as Judith Briles, the author and
management consultant, described in working with her own employees.

I   I think when you know someone has lied, we need to
give them the opportunity to open up and deal with it.
And for that I think it's important to be understanding, to
show them you want to listen and try to solve the problem. You want to help, not punish. So when you are
trying to get them to open up in this confrontation, this
is not the time to go in with a sledge hammer and hit
someone over the head with what they have done.
Rather, you want to create an atmosphere where you
convey the impression that "whatever you have to say,
it's really best to be direct with me." And that takes
tactfulness. It takes loving. It takes caring, showing your
support for the person.

Say a person has made a mistake. At first, he or she
may not want to admit it. Well, I would encourage them
to talk about it, giving them the assurance they would
not be canned. I would let them know I believe in the
possibility of change.

I had a person who worked for me who made some
mistakes in doing some things that were a bit over her
head. So I sat down with her, and I began by assuring
her: "You don't need to make excuses. Let's look at
where we are and what we need to do to make things

work for you." That way I feel she felt more free to be open, so we could deal with the problem head-on.

When to Confess or What to Do about Getting Caught

The other side of dealing with lies is, of course, deciding what to do about lying oneself—whether to tell one, whether to reveal one voluntarily, and what to do about getting caught. Again, there are no hard and fast answers, just considerations that may apply in different situations along with considerations based on personal style.

A key to dealing with personal lying is to be more conscious of these various considerations so one can determine when it might be best to use a lie, when to reveal, and how to respond when confronted by a lie, perhaps by weighing and assessing various strategic and personal-values considerations.

Although the ideal may be "don't lie," the overall reality is that at some point all of us do it. The problem is that many, if not most, of us are not really aware of how, when, or why we do it. Rather, the lie is more like an automatic defense or attack mechanism we use under various circumstances.

Thus, it may be useful to develop a management-of-lying approach so we're more conscious of when and how we do it and when it might be best to reveal lies. Ultimately, each person will have to develop his own way of approaching this, based on the situation and what he feels personally comfortable with. So this section is not designed to be a manual on how to lie! Rather, it is designed to raise final considerations and suggest the importance of being conscious about the process of lying and its results and ramifications.

Some Considerations on Whether to Lie

Some possible considerations in deciding whether to lie might include:
- the importance of the situation lied about;
- the possible gain to oneself from the lie;
- the risk of getting caught and how one feels about this;
- the potential damage to one's reputation from being caught;
- one's own personal values and morality;
- the possible benefits to others from the lie;

○ one's feelings of guilt;
○ one's feelings about getting away with the lie (i.e., will you be apt to feel guilty even if you get away with it; or would you feel relieved or glad?);
○ the existence of alternatives to the lie;
○ the likelihood that the person lied to will seek to learn the truth or will collaborate in a continuation of the lie;
○ the likelihood and the dangers of having to create other lies to cover up this one, the risk of getting caught, and the degree of penalties possible with the discovery of these future lies;
○ the way the person lied to will react if he or she discovers the lie. Will the lie be likely to be forgiven? Will there be a crisis of trust? Or perhaps an end to the relationship?

And so on. You may think of other considerations that apply for yourself. The point is to be aware of the possible gains and losses and other repercussions under the particular circumstances affecting the lie. Also, it is useful to better understand your own attitudes and values about lying to decide what is appropriate for you to do in the future.

For others, moral or spiritual considerations can be especially important, and they may find their personal values compelling. This was a major factor for Alison, the counselor. As she explained:

I   Generally, I feel like a lie is going to come back to haunt me, so that even if I get away with it now, there will still be some effect.

For some, feelings of guilt discourage the lie, even the white lie. As Roger, the philosophy teacher, reported:

I   The times I've lied, I've felt badly about it. I've felt like I was short-changing myself and the other person. I have lied to save someone's feelings, but I have felt bad about that as well.

   For example, this once happened at a conference where there was a man I was trying to impress, and he asked me what I thought of someone who I know has a good reputation with many people because he is known as a very peaceful sort of leader who works for peace. But in fact, I have not liked this person's style, because he is so evangelical. But I didn't tell this man what I really thought, because I didn't want him to think I didn't like this person when so many other people did. So I just made up a comfortable, placating answer.

But I think the man suspected that I didn't say what I was really thinking. I think he could tell I was being evasive and withholding something, and I think this created a sense of separation between us. I think it was worse to withhold something than tell him what I really wanted to say.

The most important questions for you to answer are: What are your own considerations, values, and priorities about lying? What seems to work for you?

Ultimately, you have to decide what is right for yourself.

When to Reveal or Confess the Lie

Once you have lied, should you reveal it or confess? Or is it better to keep it hidden? There is no right answer for everyone. These considerations may help you to decide:

O *How long is it since you told the original lie?* With a passage of time, it may become easier to admit it, because the other person may be more accepting.

O *How significant is the original lie to your current relationship with the person?* It may be that the revelation of the lie will disrupt the whole relationship. If so, do you feel the relationship should continue, based on this lie? Or should the relationship be reconstructed on true foundations? Are you willing to take the risk of maybe losing the relationship? Is revealing the lie important enough to take this risk?

O *How major or important was the original lie?* If trivial enough, maybe it could be ignored. But if it is so trivial, perhaps there would be little risk in revealing it.

O *How do you feel about the lie?* Do you have a strong desire to open up about it? Or are you more apt to feel: "Just let things lie. Why rock the boat?"

O *How likely is the lie to come out if you don't reveal it?* This might be a reason to reveal it first. Then you can better control the revelation, and the repercussions may be easier on you.

O *How is the person you have lied to likely to respond?* Is he or she likely to appreciate your candor, to be forgiving? Or is he or she more likely to be upset, perhaps even end the relationship? And how much better is it likely to be if you reveal the lie yourself rather than have the person find out? What is the risk of discovery if you do not tell? And how important is it to you to reveal the lie if the person reacts badly to it?

O *What would be the best way to make the revelation?* Would you prefer to explain in a letter what happened? Would you rather just come right out with the lie? If so, what would be the best way to do this? In person? On the phone? At their home? At yours? In an office setting?

Sometimes the pressures to reveal can become complex, such as when there are conflicting considerations such as a moral imperative against lying combined with a realization of the potential losses that telling can bring. This dilemma occurred to a friend of Don's, the engineer. As Don told me:

> My friend had herpes, and he had started this relationship with a woman. Well, in the beginning he didn't want to announce it. After all, they had just started to date, didn't have an intimate relationship, and this wasn't the kind of thing one announces to the world.
>
> But as the relationship started to get serious, he felt he had a need to tell her, because now this was something she should know. Yet, at the same time, he dreaded telling her, because he knew this might be the end of the relationship.
>
> Well, he agonized over this for many days. But finally he decided he needed to tell. So he told her, and that blew the whole relationship. Morally and ethically, he felt he had to do it, and then it was up to her to decide if the relationship would continue.

The Role of Forgiveness

If you find that someone has lied to you or someone confesses a lie, how willing are you to forgive? There seem to be general patterns in how people respond to lies and are willing to forgive.

O *If the lie isn't too serious,* especially if it just happens once, whether confessed or revealed, there is a tendency to forgive and let bygones be bygones.

O *If the lies are only occasional ones,* particularly in the beginning of a relationship, usually the person lied to will forgive. Why? Because people recognize that others might sometimes lie as a kind of convenience or because people weren't totally consistent or perfect in their statements and behavior. But then, if people started to show a pattern of lying, that's when the victims would start to be unforgiving, because the repeated lies would undermine their ability to trust the person and count on the relationship.

0 *If a person starts to lie consistently or shows a pattern of lies,* then it becomes hard to forgive. For every person, of course, the tolerance point is different—just when do a few lies turn into a pattern? But once they do, that's when people start to become unwilling to forgive.

0 *Forgiveness is encouraged if the liar shows a sense of remorse* or a willingness to change. Again, people differ widely in how much they are wiling to accept another person's remorse or expressed desire to change, but this kind of attitude can help to cushion the effects of the lie and promote healing.

At some point forgiveness is necessary, though hard to do, because otherwise the hate and hostility generated by the lie could be self-destructive. For example, Frances, the computer-systems supervisor, had this kind of experience when she continued to feel hostility to two men she had been involved with who used lies and unfulfilled promises to get money out of her, which they never repaid. As she described it:

> Eventually, I forgave those two people for what they did to me, and they came back in my life and established a kind of friendship. But before then, when I still felt that hate, it ate at me, and I learned that this hate didn't really hurt them—it hurts me. It hurts with the emotional pain, and I know it contributes to things like cancer and stress. So I felt better when I gave it up.

Finally, there is the question of self-forgiveness. Can you forgive yourself after you've either lied or have felt duped by having someone lie to you? This can be equally important to the process of healing.

Toward a Solution in Dealing with Lying

Given the pervasiveness of lying and its paradoxical nature, what should we do about it?

I think we need to be aware of this dual nature and come to be more clear about when lying may be constructive and when it may be dangerous. In general, I think we need to make a commitment to the truth and integrity, where it is at all possible to do this, including in these everyday social situations where the so-

called social lie is so common. For example, tactful but true explanations might be used to turn down invitations. At the same time we
need to recognize that lies to help social relations may be more
beneficial than the truth, such as when the assurances of "you'll get
better" will help a person heal, though the outcome may seem
uncertain and more probably grim. And to facilitate social
relationships, we may need to look the other way when we know or
suspect others have lied to us.

On the other hand, we also need to be aware when lies become
serious and disruptive, when they threaten bonds of trust, and seek to
avoid such lies ourselves as well as be ready to handle such lies by
others. In short, we need this awareness so we can make choices and
manage the lying we encounter in our lives.

To some extent, this process may be conscious and analytical,
based on assessing, evaluating, and choosing. But part of it is
intuitive, based in effect on listening to yourself and following that
"little voice" within.

To help you decide what to do, consider the following:

Look at the Whys Behind the Lie

It may be that the lies are covering up some important truth or
hidden negative feelings that would be better revealed. A good
example of this might be the person who comes to work constantly late and then makes excuses. He could be doing this because he really doesn't like the job. So if you're the one who's
lying about the situation, maybe you have to look at whether this
is the right job for you. If you're the supervisor, you should
discuss this with the person who is lying and try to find his
reasons. Maybe there is something in the office that could be
changed so he feels better about the job.

If there are lies in a relationship, it might be good to see what
these are saying about the relationship, particularly if it has been
a good one. Certainly, breaking up the relationship over the lie is
one possibility, but maybe looking at the underlying reasons for
the lie might be a way of renewing or rebuilding it. If the lie is
brought up and addressed and the problems resolved, the lie
could lead to healing.

Be Ready to Call People on Their Lies

Let people know the lies are not okay. Otherwise, this suggests you
either aren't aware of them or are willing to accept them,

which only encourages more lies, and can leave you feeling resentful.

Create a Supportive Environment for Truth Telling

Creating a supportive environment for those who have lied can make it safe for them to reveal or explain their lies. If the lies are designed to cover up failure in the workplace, it may be important to give people permission to acknowledge failure and acknowledge they are not perfect. By giving people this space to see that their failures, mistakes, or weaknesses can be forgiven or will be treated like learning experiences, it takes away some of the fear and insecurity that causes the lies.

Tell the Truth to Yourself

It is important to tell the truth to yourself, even if it is initially painful, because that self-awareness is the beginning step to self-healing.

Marketing and management-consultant Robert Middleton put it very well when he observed that:

> Telling the truth to yourself is transformational. It is crucial to say the way things really are and really work, instead of creating some pretense as to how we think things ought to be, hope it should be, or wish it would be.
>
> If we really tell the truth about ourselves, what's in it for us is aliveness and satisfaction and joy and love and understanding and connection. It helps us build bridges to others, and it contributes to our ultimate success. And we discover who we really are and what we are. So telling the truth is very powerful.

Use the Truth for Building & Healing Relationships

Telling the truth can be healing. Relationship-counselor Susan Scott has advocated these benefits in assisting her clients toward more honest relationships based on personal integrity. As she told me:

> I think people should adopt the cardinal rule of telling the truth. That's how you heal everything that's hap-

pened in the past in relationships. And by telling the truth to yourself as well as to others, that's how you get or create for yourself what it is that you really want and need in the future generally, and in relationships. So telling the truth can add to your own self-esteem and the quality of life.

On the other hand, if there are lies in a relationship, I think it's important to clean it up or the lies will always be there between the people. Yes, there may be a risk of breaking up the relationship if the lie comes out. But if the lie remains, the relationship isn't going to last anyway. Because the truth always comes out.

Recognize the Long-term Advantages of Being Committed to the Truth

Finally, recognize that in the long run, a commitment to truth does pay off. There may be short-term gains for many lies, but there is always the risk that lies will come out, and in the meantime, they can create guilt and anxiety. People in business, for example, have found that a long-term orientation toward integrity and service is what makes a business strong, and this kind of larger commitment not only helps the individual business but also the economy as a whole.

I think most of us can agree that the last decade's focus on greed and all manner of manipulation, including lies, helped to contribute to the economic crisis we now face.

Similarly, lies and cover-ups have proved dangerous in the development of science and technology (witness the failure of the Challenger space shuttle, the errors in the Hubble telescope, and the continued seepage of retroviruses into the blood supply).

In short, what I am suggesting is that we need to recognize and embrace the value of truth and integrity, while realizing that in some circumstances there may be benefits to using lies to a limited degree or letting the lies of others pass.

When we encounter lying or consider lying ourselves, we should control how we deal with lying, combining a sense of awareness with an understanding of the pros and cons and issues involved. Using intuition and listening to that inner voice will then help us decide what to do. With this combination of awareness, reason, and intuition, we can take charge and better choose how to deal with lying in everyday life.

What's Your Lie-Q?

(Lying Quotient)

*T*his simple quiz does not aspire to provide a serious scientific evaluation of your character in matters of lying. It does try, though—in an entertaining way—to make you aware of your propensity not to tell the truth in different situations of your personal, social, and professional life. Answer the questions *honestly*. Then add up the numbers in the circles corresponding to your answers and look up your score (on a scale of 0-285) on the key at the end of the quiz.

1. Give yourself the number of points indicated for your response to the following statements about lying.

   a. It is always wrong to tell a lie.

Yes	(0)
No	(2)
Not sure	(1)

   b. It is all right to lie, as long as the lie doesn't harm anyone.

Yes	(2)
No	(0)
Not sure	(1)

SUBTOTAL

c. It is never right to tell a lie that will harm anyone.   _____
                Yes   (0)
                No   (2)
                Not sure   (1)

d. It is all right to lie in order to protect oneself from harm.   _____
                Yes   (2)
                Yes, but only if it is   (1)
                  really serious harm
                No   (0)
                Not sure   (1)

e. It is all right to lie to hurt someone else if that person has
   done something to hurt one.   _____
                Yes   (2)
                Yes, but only if that person has (1)
                  done one very serious harm
                No   (0)
                Not sure   (1)

f. It is all right to lie in order to protect someone else from
                                                            being hurt.
                Yes   (2)
                Yes, but only if that person   (1)
                  will be hurt very seriously
                No   (0)
                Not sure   (1)

g. It is all right to lie to become successful or gain an advantage, as long as no one else will be hurt by that lie.   _____
                Yes   (2)
                No   (0)
                Not sure   (1)

h. It is all right to lie to become successful or gain an advantage, because that's the way life is, and so it's necessary to
   do it.   _____
                Yes   (2)
                No   (0)
                Not sure   (1)

i. It is all right to lie when the benefit to be gained outweighs
   the harm to result from that lie.   _____
                Yes   (2)
                No   (0)
                Not sure   (1)

SUBTOTAL   (_____)

2. What are the main reasons you would tell a lie? (Rate your biggest reasons with a 2; your occasional reasons with a 1; and reasons when you would never tell a lie with a 0.)

To protect someone from harm	(x 1=)
To cover up an embarrassing situation	(X 2=)
To avoid punishment	(x 2=)
To make someone feel good	(x 1 =)
To get revenge	(X 3=)
To get a job	(x 1=)
To get a promotion	(x 2=)
To get more money	(x 2=)
To get out of an undesired social obligation	(x 1=)
To further your reputation	(X 1=)
To escape blame for a mistake	(X 2=)
To put the blame on someone else	(x 3=)
To conceal your age	(x 1 =)
To seem more successful	(X 1 =)
To do better on a test	(X 2=)
To obtain a contract	(x 2=)
To make a better deal in business	(x 2=)
To sell something to someone	(X 2=)
To pay less for something	(x 2=)
To have or cover up an affair	(X 3=)
To protect a member of your family	(X 1=)
To make someone you don't like look bad	(x 3=)
To hide an unpleasant truth about yourself	(x 2=)
To get out of paying a ticket	(x 2=)
To avoid being accused of something you did	(X 3=)
To cut through some bureaucracy more quickly	(x 1=)
To seem younger than you are	(x 1 =)
To get ahead in line	(x 2=)
To get into someplace without paying	(X 2=)
To keep someone from knowing information they shouldn't know.	(x 2=)
To get a date	(X 1=)
To make the results of a project come out as desired(	x 2=)
To keep someone from knowing something bad (e.g., an illness)	(x 1=)
To let someone think you like something when you don't	(x 1 =)
To have a better sexual relationship (or to get sex)	(x 2=)
To get out of doing something with someone you don't want to do something with	(x 2=)
To convince someone that your position is right	(x 2=)

SUBTOTAL

3. Indicate on a scale of 0-3 how often you might lie to each of the following types of people. (0 = never; 1 = rarely; 2 = occasionally; 3 = often.)

salesmen
customers or clients
police officers
clerks
business associates
employers
employees
friends
relatives
parents
children
neighbors
priest/minister/rabbi
lovers
spouse
pollsters
reporters
therapist/counselor
teachers
students
business partners   _____

SUBTOTAL

4. How many lies have you told in the last week?   _____
        None   (0)
        1-4   (1)
        5-9   (2)
        10 or more   (3)

5. How may lies have you told in the past day (or yesterday, if it's still early)?
        None   (0)
        1-4   (1)
        3-4   (2)
        5 or more   (3)

~~Now, total up your points from~~ the five circles to get your Lie-Q!   _____

Scoring Key

I 0-24   A Model of Absolute Integrity—but are you for real? You seem too honest to be believed.

25-49   A **Real** Straight Shooter—**most** of the time. Flexibly honest.

50-99 A Pragmatic Fibber

100-149 A Real Pinocchio

150-199 A Compulsive Liar—you probably cheated on this test.

200+   Someone Who Will **Lie about Almost Everything**—are you reading this in prison or on *Prime Time?*

References

Introduction

1 Merrill McLoughlin with Jeffrey L. Sheier and Gordon Witkin, "A Nation of Liars?" U.S. *News and World Report,* February 23, 1987, pp. 54-59.

2 *Ibid.,* p. 59.

3 Allan Halcrow, "Is There a Crisis in Business Ethics?" *Personnel Journal,* Vol. 66, Issue 11, November 1987, pp. 10-17.

4 McLoughlin, Sheier, and Witkin, "A Nation of Liars?" U.S. *News and World Report,* February 23, 1987, p. 55.

5 *Ibid.,* p. 54.

6 *Ibid.,* p. 56.

7 Taught by Jeffrey Masson and Daidie Donnelly. Masson has recently published a book, *The Assault on Truth,* dealing with looking at issues of authenticity in one's own psyche. Masson previously got into trouble for telling too much about what he found in the Freud Archives when he was a director and revealing some of the lies he claims were told by Freud. Masson is continuing to confront the psychiatric establishment about what he claims are its hidden truths about the real Freud.

Chapter 1

1 Sissela Bok, *Lying: Moral Choice in Public and Private Life,* New York: Vintage House, 1978, p. 17.

2 Thomas E. Carson, "On the Definition of Lying: A Reply to Jones and Revisions," *Journal of Business Ethics,* 1988, p. 509.

3 Harry Frankfurt, "Reflections on Bullshit," *Harper's Magazine,* Vol. 274, February 1987, pp. 14-15.

4 Erica E. Goode, "Nature's Knaves and Tricksters: Some Animals Show a Penchant for Dissembling and Deceit," *U.S. News and World Report,* October 23, 1989, pp. 6163.

5 *Ibid.,* p. 62.

6 *Ibid.*

7 R. W. Bryne and A. Whitten, "Tactical Deception of Familiar Individuals in Baboons," *Animal Behavior,* Vol. 33, No. 2, May 1985, pp. 669-673.

8 As recounted by Joseph Campbell in the PBS film of his lecture series: "Transformation of Myth through Time."

9 R. H. Wiley, "The Evolution of Communication: Information and Manipulation," T. R. Halliday and P. J. B. Slater (eds.) *Communication Behavior,* Vol. 2, New York: Freeman, 1983.

10 Charles F. Bond, Jr., Karen Nelson Kahler, and Lucia M. Paolicelli, "The Miscommunication of Deception: An Adaptive Perspective," *Journal of Experimental Social Psychology,* 1985, pp. 331-345.

11 *Ibid.,* pp. 332-333.

12 Michael P. Carroll, "The Trickster as Self-Buffoon and Culture Hero," *Ethos,* Vol. 12, 105-131.

13 Francis E. Kazemek, Muriel Radebaugh, and Pat Rigg, "Old

Man Coyote Makes the World: Using Native American Tales," *English Journal,* Vol. 76, February 1987, pp. 100-105.

14 William Manson, "Trickster's Triumph: Sublimation and Culture," *The Journal of Psychohistory,* Vol. 15, No. 3, Winter 1988, pp. 325-332.

15 Kazemek, Radebaugh, and Rigg, *op. cit.,* p. 102.

16 Manson, *op. cit.,* p. 325.

17 Claudia V. Camp, "Wise and Strange: An Interpretation of the Female Imagery in Proverbs in Light of Trickster Mythology," *Semia,* No. 42,1988, pp. 14-36.

18   Naomi Steinberg, "Israelite Tricksters, Their Analogues and Cross-Cultural Study," *Semia,* No. 42, 1988, pp. 1-13.

19 Joseph E. Brown, "The Wisdom of the Contrary," interview by D. M. Dooling, *Parabola: The Magazine of Myth and Tradition,* Vol. 4, No. 1,1979, pp. 54-65.

20 Ingvild Saelid Gilhus, "The Gnostic Demiurge—An Agnostic Trickster," *Religion: Journal of Religion and Religions,* Vol. 14, October 1984, pp. 301-311.

21 *Ibid.,* p. 307.

22 St. Augustine, "Lying," *Treatises on Various Subjects* in R. J. Deferari, ed., *Fathers of the Church,* New York: Catholic University of America Press, 1952, Vol. 14, Chapter 14.

23 St. Augustine, "The Enchiridion," in Sissela Bok, *Lying: Moral Choice in Public and Private Life,* New York: Vintage Books, 1978, p. 34.

24 Thomas Aquinas, *Summa Theologica* 2.2, qus. 110, art. 2.

25 Immanuel Kant, *Critique of Pure Reason and Other Writings in Moral Philosophy,* ed. and trans. Lewis White Beck, Chicago: University of Chicago Press, 1949, pp. 346

349; quoted in Mark Dratch, "Nothing But the Truth?" *Judaism: A Quarterly Journal,* Vol. 37, Spring, 1988, pp. 218-228.

26 Hugo Grotius, *On the Law of War and Peace,* trans. F. M. Kelsy and others, Indianapolis: Bobbs Merrill Co. 1925, bk. 3, ch. 1, quoted in Dratch, "Nothing But the Truth?" p. 219.

27 H. Sidgwick, *The Methods of Ethics,* London: Macmillan and Company, 1907, p. 316, quoted in Dratch, "Nothing But the Truth?" p. 219.

28 Mark Dratch, "Nothing But the Truth?" *Judaism: A Quarterly Journal,* Vol. 37. Spring 1988,218-228.

29 Dafna Allon, "Reflections on the Art of Lying," *Commentary,* Vol. 81, No. 6, June 1986,47-54.

30 Ann Landers, "The Third Biggest Lie," *San Francisco Examiner* (from the Los Angeles Times Syndicate and Creators Syndicate).

31 Daniel Goleman, "The Truth about Liars," *San Francisco Chronicle,* 1988.

32 *Ibid.*

33 Charles V. Ford, Bryan H. King, and Marc H. Hollender, "Lies and Liars: Psychiatric Aspects of Prevarication," *American Journal of Psychiatry,* Vol. 145, No. 5, May 1988, pp. 554-562.

34 Mark Hosenball, "The Culture of Lying," *The New Republic,* July 13 & 20,1987, pp. 16-18.

35 "The Truth about Lying (Views of Beverly Palmer)", *USA Today,* Vol. 116, December 1987, pp. 3-4.

Chapter 2

1 Elizabeth Kamarch Minnich, "Why Not Lie?" *Soundings: An Interdisciplinary Journal,* Vol. 68, No. 4, Winter 1985, pp. 493-508.

2 *Ibid.*

Chapter 3

1   Ervin Coffman, *The Presentation of Self in Everyday Life,* New York: Doubleday, 1959.

Chapter 6

1 Owen Edwards, "Thrice-Told Tales," *The New York Times Magazine,* March 20, 1988, p. 16.

2   *Ibid.*

3   *Ibid.,* p. 17.

Chapter 8

1   The book describing this research is *Erotic Power,* published by Citadel Press.

2   Her books previously cited include *Women to Women: From Sabotage to Support* and *The Confidence Factor.*

Chapter 9

1 Estimates and questionnaire results on the percent of married individuals having affairs vary widely—anywhere from 10 to 70 percent. I have used 30 to 50 percent as the more conservative middle-range figures that are more widely agreed upon by those in the field.

Chapter 10

1   Paul Ekman, Why *Kids Lie,* New York: Macmillan Publishing Company, 1989.

2 Paul Ekman, "Would a Child Lie?" *Psychology Today,* July—August 1989, p. 62.

3   *Ibid.*

4   *Ibid.,* p. 65.

Chapter 11

1   Daniel Coleman, *Vital Lies, Simple Truths: The Psychology of Self-Deception,* New York: Simon and Schuster, 1985.

2   *Ibid.,* p. 22.

3   *Ibid.,* p. 32.

4   *Ibid.,* p. 37.

5   *Ibid.,* p. 39.

6   *Ibid.,* pp. 52-

7   53. *Ibid.,* p. 90.

8   *Ibid* p. 98.

9   *Ibid.,* p. 100.

Chapter 12

1   Charles F. Bond, Jr., Karen Nelson Kahler, and Lucia M. Paolicelli.   "The Miscommunication of Deception: An Adaptive Perspective." *Journal of Experimental Social Psychology,* Vol. 21, 1985, pp. 331-345.

2   *Ibid.,* p. 341.

3 R. E. Kraut, "Humans as Lie Detectors: Some Second Thoughts," *Journal of Communication,* Vol. 39, 1980, pp. 209-216.

4 Bond, et al., "The Miscommunication of Deception," 1985, p. 241.

5 R. E. Kraut and D. Poe, "On the Line: The Deception Judgments of Customs Inspectors and Laymen," *Journal of Personality and Social Psychology,* Vol. 39, 1980, pp. 784-798.

6 Bond, et al., "The Miscommunication of Deception," 1985, p. 341.

7   Charles F. Bond, Jr., and William E. Fahey, "False Suspicion and the Misperception of Deceit," *British Journal of Social Psychology,* Vol. 26, 1987, pp. 41-46.

8   Bruce Bower, "Sales Pitches: The Lies Have It," *Science News,* Vol. 134, August 27, 1988, p. 140. Charles F. Bond, Jr., and William E. Fahey, "False Suspicion and the Misperception of Deceit," *op. cit.*

9 Bella M. DePaulo, Julie I. Stone, and G. Daniel Lassiter. "Telling Ingratiating Lies: Effects of Target Sex and Target Attractiveness on Verbal and Nonverbal Deceptive Success," *Journal of Personality and Social Psychology,* Vol. 48, May 1985; No. 5, pp. 1191-1203.

10 *Ibid.*

11 *Ibid.,* pp. 1200-1201.

12 Paul Ekman, *Telling Lies: Clues to Deceit in the Marketplace, Politics, and Marriage,* New York: W. W. Norton & Company, 1985, p. 39.
13 *Ibid.,* p. 43.
14 *Ibid.,* p. 44.
15 *Ibid.*
16 *Ibid.,* p. 79.
17 *Ibid.,* pp. 47-48.
18 *Ibid.,* p. 51.
19 *Ibid.*
20 *Ibid.,* p. 60.
21 *Ibid.,* p. 65.
22 *Ibid.,* p. 70.
23 *Ibid.,* p. 78.
24 *Ibid.,* pp. 81-82.
25 *Ibid.,* p. 84.
26 *Ibid.,* p. 85.
27 *Ibid.*
28 *Ibid.,* p. 88.
29 *Ibid.,* p. 90.
30 *Ibid.,* p. 91.
31 *Ibid.,* p. 92-93.
32 *Ibid.*
33 *Ibid.,* pp. 102-103.
34 *Ibid.,* p. 105-107.
35 *Ibid.,* p. 109-113.
36 *Ibid.,* p. 114.
37 *Ibid.,* p. 115.
38 *Ibid.,* p. 123.
39 *Ibid.,* p. 124.
40 *Ibid.,* p. 126.
41 *Ibid.,* p. 129.
42 *Ibid.,* p. 131.
43 *Ibid.,* p. 142.
44 *Ibid.,* p. 143.
45 *Ibid.*
46 *Ibid.,* p. 142-143.
47 John Leo, "The Fine Art of Catching Liars," *Time,* April 22, 1985, p. 59. Also, Ekman, *Telling Lies, op. cit.,* p. 146.
48 *Ibid.,* p. 59. Also, Ekman, *Telling Lies, op. cit.,* p 146.
49 Valerie Adler, "Lying Smiles," *Psychology Today,* Vol. 22, July-August, 1988, p. 16. From Ekman's article: Paul Ekman, Wallace V. Friesen, and Maureen O'Sullivan, "Smiles When Lying," *Journal of Personality and Social Psychology,* Vol. 54, No. 3, March 1988, pp. 414 420.
50 Ekman, *Telling Lies, op. cit.,* p. 149.

Gini Graham Scott, Ph.D., is a nationally known writer, consultant, speaker, and seminar/workshop leader, specializing in business and work relationships and professional and personal development. She is the founder of Changemakers and Creative Communications & Research, and has published over 40 books on diverse subjects. Recent books include *A Survival Guide for Working with Bad Bosses* and *A Survival Guide for Working with Humans,* both from AMACOM, and *Resolving Conflict, Mind Power,* and *The Empowered Mind* from iUniverse, Inc. Scott has received national media exposure for her books, including appearances on *Good Morning America, Oprah, Montel Williams,* and CNN. Her Website is www.ginigrahamscott.com.

www.ingramcontent.com/pod-product-compliance
Lightning Source LLC
Chambersburg PA
CBHW060246290526
45789CB00001B/209